HUNTING IN A FARMER'S WORLD

Praise for Hunting in a Farmer's World

"How Refreshing! A celebration of the drivers of our economy. This book is clarifying, validating and incredibly helpful. A must for any entrepreneur."

—Gino Wickman, CEO, EOS Worldwide, author of *Traction* and creator of the Entrepreneurial Operating System (EOS®)

"I loved it. In order to leave a successful business, it first has to be successful. Hunting in a Farmer's World explains to entrepreneurs that they don't have to follow the requirements of traditional management books to succeed. It encourages the hunters of the business world to do what they do best...hunt!"

—John Brown, CEO, the Business Enterprise Institute, author of *How to Run Your Business So You can Leave it in Style* and *Cash Out, Move On!*

"If you want to know what makes an entrepreneur, what entrepreneurs do, what they don't do, whether you're wasting your time and money posing as one, or if you actually possess the primordial "hunter" DNA to be one, congratulations. You've come to the right place. In classic, no nonsense fashion, John F. Dini lays all of it out so you can determine whether to take the entrepreneurial road less traveled and go against the odds, or start working on your farmer resume."

—Jim Blasingame, Host of *The Small Business Advocate®* Show, author of *Small Business is Like a Bunch of Bananas* and *Three Minutes to Success*

HUNTING IN
A FARMER'S
WORLD

CELEBRATING THE MIND OF AN ENTREPRENEUR

JOHN F. DINI

Gardendale Press

Published by Gardendale Press
12015 Radium Street
San Antonio, TX 78216

Printed in the United States of America

Library of Congress Control Number: 2013946801

ISBN-10: 0-9790531-1-0
ISBN-13: 978-0-9790531-1-5

First Printing: September 2013
10 9 8 7 6 5 4 3

This book is dedicated to the hunters.

Content

Acknowledgements

Some authors put the acknowledgements at the end of a book, but there is something I wanted you to know up front.

All of the stories in this book are true. In only one case, the business owner asked that I use a pseudonym. The rest are real names, real owners, and real life. They are the people who made this book possible. I cannot thank them enough for sharing the stories of their challenges and successes.

My thanks (and my love) to my wife, Leila, who has been my rock; the much-needed anchor that has kept me from spinning off into space for almost forty years.

Like any venture, this was a team effort. My staff stepped up as they always do. Christi Brendlinger, Beth Sorenson and Sarah Salgado took on the duties of layout and graphics, web design, proofreading and editing, and contributing a lot of good ideas as we progressed. (Not to mention handling their normal duties along the way.)

To Jim Blasingame of *The Small Business Advocate*®, whose enthusiasm for this book encouraged me to think bigger. To Michael Gerber, who gave me some very direct coaching at a critical time, and caused me to go the extra mile in making it better. To both men, whose work has also helped so many thousands of entrepreneurs.

Lara August and her talented team at Robot Creative took the time to understand where I was going, and designed cover and interior art that brought home my message.

Finally, my thanks to Allen Fishman, the founder of The Alternative Board®, who offered me an opportunity to work with hundreds of business owners, and to join with other coaches and clients who feel as passionately about free enterprise as I do. The thousands of hours I've spent with them are reflected on every page of this book.

Style note

I am not gender biased, but writing around politically correct usage of both male and female pronouns gets old, and disrupts the rhythm of a sentence. I refer to both where it seems appropriate, but more often default to the male pronoun for better flow. Most of the successful female entrepreneurs that I know understand that they work in a male dominated business environment, and shrug it off. I have no intention of slighting or demeaning female owners. A hunter is a hunter.

Introduction

Hunters hunt.

I was representing an owner in the sale of his small technical services company. The Great Recession was just beginning. Half of our potential buyers had just watched their stock portfolios shrink dramatically. The rest were frightened that the business would go into a steep decline the day after they bought it.

The man sitting across the conference room table from me was the best prospect we had seen so far. In his mid-fifties, he had just accepted a buyout from his Fortune 500 employer, giving him ample cash to purchase a small business. He had an employment history of advancement through increasing levels of management responsibility. He knew the industry and had many personal connections in it that he could leverage to grow the business.

I was going through my normal qualifying questions; even though I was pretty convinced we had found our ideal new owner for this company. "Why do you want to buy this business?" I asked.

"For almost thirty years, I've had a burning passion to own my own business," he said. "I have always itched to be my own boss. It is all that I've ever really wanted."

My heart sank. This was not our guy. We went through all the steps of the selling process anyway, but in the end he backed out because he got "a job offer he couldn't refuse" from another large corporation.

He was not a hunter. No one takes thirty years to act on a "burning passion." Building a business isn't just an "itch." Entrepreneurs are driven to hunt and win. Some are born, some choose to be entrepreneurs and some stumble into it by circumstance. Not all entrepreneurs own a business, and not all business owners are entrepreneurs. But entrepreneurs are the hunters of the 21st century and they all have specific traits in common.

Entrepreneurs hunt. Managers farm.

Bringing in new sources of revenue is hunting. Finding and training great employees is hunting. Closing deals is hunting. Outmaneuvering a competitor is hunting. Motivating people to excel is hunting.

Management is farming. Balancing the checkbook is farming. Paying the rent is farming. Locking up the business at night or opening it in the morning is farming. Purchasing supplies is farming. Writing procedures is farming.

This is a book about the mind of an entrepreneur. I have spent my life working with hunters. I understand what drives them and what holds them back. Entrepreneurs come in many flavors; some own businesses and some work for other people. Others dedicate themselves to community service, and many just live their lives with an entrepreneurial attitude. We will discuss them in the context of business ownership because it is the most identifiable expression of entrepreneurial characteristics, but if you are a hunter this book is for you.

You and I will range in our discussion from what makes a hunter to the challenges faced by most entrepreneurs. We generally follow a chronology of a successful entrepreneurial career, from hiring the first employee to exiting the business. Along the way, we will offer guidance about how to resist the influence of farmers, and run your business in a way that works best for you. We approach the critical components of entrepreneurship, including leadership, management and handling success, from different angles at different places in the book.

This isn't organized as a step-by-step manual, but then I'm not a step-by-step kind of guy. The odds are that you probably aren't one either—if you are a hunter.

Prologue: 7,000 BC

His thighs ached from squatting in the bushes in the cold rain, but he didn't dare to change his position. They had wounded the giant deer just before nightfall, when they had surprised it at the watering hole. It had broken through their ring during the night but they could track it with hearing and smell almost as if it was broad daylight.

The hunters needed to see the quarry in order to finish it off, but the morning had raised a thick, almost impenetrable fog. Now the animal was silent and the hunters were even quieter. If it bolted, it could take days to track it down, and the rest of the tribe didn't have days to wait for fresh food. If the hunters rushed it without knowing exactly where it was, another man might fall to the twelve-foot antlers, just as one had last night.

He shifted his weight slightly to his other haunch. He hoped that he would still be able to move quickly when the moment for action arrived.

He was Hunter. He wasn't the strongest man in the tribe or the fastest. He simply had the greatest ability to focus on the task of hunting. He could ignore pain and fatigue like no other in the tribe. He would hunt through any weather and under any conditions. He never came back empty handed.

The other men followed his commands. He had taught them to work together and they were far more successful than when they had just been a disorganized mob. Now the faster ones stayed to the outside to limit the game's ability to get around them. The stronger ones were in the middle where their spear thrusts could be concentrated for greater effect. Hunter sometimes wondered why the others couldn't solve problems and see the obvious like he could.

He wasn't the chief of his tribe. They didn't have a formal system of selection but, for a while, he had begun giving directions and people listened to him. It didn't last very long. He didn't like having the others come to him with their arguments and disagreements. When he was gone on a hunt it seemed no one else in the tribe made any decisions. He began asking another man, Tanner, what he thought about things.

Soon, everyone else went to Tanner, and Hunter was left alone to do what he did best.

Off to his left, a twig snapped. He knew it wasn't one of his hunters; he had trained them too well. The deer was closer than he had thought.

Hunter saw a shadow in the fog where the noise had originated. It was the deer. It was time. He rose, ignoring the screaming of his muscles and praying to the hunting gods that his joints didn't crack. He moved forward, one step, then another. The deer was looking the other way.

It was huge, one of the biggest he had seen. Seven feet at the shoulder, with the jugular vein almost nine feet off the ground. Hunter slowly looked to either side. His nearest companion was too far away for a coordinated attack. A thrown spear might miss. He needed to get closer, and he would only get one thrust.

Another step and the deer, sensing his presence, began to turn its head. Two quick, silent steps, a leap, and he drove the spear deep into its neck.

The deer swung its massive head and Hunter fell back to avoid the sweeping antlers. The animal bolted, but by now the other hunters were in full-throated pursuit. It was mortally wounded. They would chase it down and finish it, then cut it up to carry back to the tribe.

Others would prepare the meat and use the skin and bones for clothing and tools. A giant deer made the tribe temporarily wealthy. Hunter's work was done … for today.

PART I: On Being a Hunter

Chapter 1
What is a Hunter?

SINCE THE DAWN OF TIME, hunters have provided for others. As soon as humans learned how to use a sharp stick, hunting delivered the protein that made them smarter and stronger. Every advance in society, from basic shelter to written language, was first possible because a hunter provided the nourishment that allowed others to organize, and eventually to farm.

At first, every man and woman had to hunt for his or her own survival. The emergence of the Hunter, the person in a tribe who specialized in tracking and killing enough game to feed others, defined a critical shift in human development. Hunters had to be focused, pursuing their goals in spite of weather or fatigue. They were creative. As the game learned to be more wary, the Hunter needed to think up new techniques. They were accountable. Hunters knew that what they did meant the survival and prosperity of many others who could not hunt.

Hunting vs. Farming

Entrepreneurs are the hunters of the 21st century. There are 26 million small businesses (those with fewer than 500 employees) in the United States. Of those, about 9 million have more than one employee. Those 9 million small business owners provide over 60%, and by some government estimates as much as 75%, of all the new job creation in America. They meet payroll for four out of every ten jobs in the nation. That means 3% of the population is delivering the means to work, eat, and play to a huge portion of the wage earners in the largest economy in the world. They are the hunters.

Most books about running a small business ignore this reality. They tell hunters how to be farmers. Hundreds of "management experts" tell you that you are doing it incorrectly. They say that you need to have more systems, more processes, and more management. They tell you to rein in your inspiration and apply analysis to your instincts. They teach that the way to business success is for a hunter to become a farmer.

They are wrong.

Business authors can easily dissect a big corporation where there are hundreds or thousands of well-documented data points. Multiple employees are subjected to the same motivational techniques, receive similar performance evaluations, or have reward systems designed to reach nearly identical goals. That makes large organizations measurable and renders plenty of material about what works and what doesn't.

On the other hand, an author can't invest his time in a book about a rapidly growing small company, only to stop halfway through with an ending that says, "Then the key salesman quit and sales went downhill from there." As a result, business authors typically write about businesses where information is easily collected, and their conclusions are supported by quantifiable evidence.

There is a problem with using big business models to develop management lessons for small businesses. The success of a small company is determined by how well it satisfies its owners' needs. Successful entrepreneurial businesses are not built by imitating the processes used to manage thousands of people, or by learning how to effectively utilize millions of dollars in resources. Hunters build them.

Hunters create; they don't manage

Managing a large organization is farming. Hunters don't farm; they hunt. They may make farming possible, but they aren't farmers themselves. That is why entrepreneurs buy millions of books on business, and then fail to implement much of the advice in them.

It isn't that "business farming" is wrong; management techniques, systems, policies and procedures just aren't what a *hunter* should be doing to build a successful business.

Entrepreneurs create; they don't manage. They build with ideas, not with policy manuals. They solve problems as they arise, because planning will inevitably fail to anticipate the next problem. They make money by being faster and smarter than the forces arrayed against them (and there are many). They don't succeed by carefully charting long-term incremental improvements. That is the province of large corporations.

What Do You Do?

People ask, "What do you do?" A business owner answers in the first person. "We manufacture widgets for the chemical industry," or "I distribute cleaning supplies to janitorial companies." Entrepreneurs describe a lifestyle, not a job. An entrepreneur's answers are comprehensive, encompassing the entire company and his relationship to it.

Employees say, "I am a supervisor in a plant that manufactures widgets," or "I call on janitorial companies for a cleaning supply wholesaler." Those with a job answer specifically about their duties as an employee.

Sometimes the questioner doesn't get it. They press for information that is more specific. "Oh, well that is what your company does. What do you do?" Every owner takes pride and satisfaction in answering, "It is my company. I run it. That is what I do." If you are a business owner, your business is integrated as part of your identity.

We all attend family gatherings from time to time. The ceremonies of life—weddings, funerals, graduations and birthdays—bring us together with family and friends. At a wedding reception, you are introduced to a distant cousin whom you haven't seen since childhood. The introduction probably includes your status as a business owner. "Do you remember little Cousin Bobby? He has his own company now." Perhaps you hear it as you pass by a group of aunts in conversation; "There goes Rebecca. Did you know that she wound up owning her own business?"

You know what they are thinking. It may be the somewhat awed tone of being in the presence of success, or a "Who would believe it?" skepticism. When you are a business owner among non-owners, the undercurrent of envy and admiration comes from certain commonly held beliefs about the lifestyle of a business owner.

You pay yourself as much as you want. As the holder of the checkbook, you can just decide how much salary you need, and take it. After all, you determine other people's compensation, so you can also determine your own, right?

You only work as much as you want. No one tells you to be in the office by a particular time. No one orders you to stay at your desk until a deadline is met. You can't be fired for leaving early. You don't have to accrue vacation. If you work a lot of hours, it's probably just because you like money so much. (See belief number one, above.)

You only do what you like to do. That's why you have employees. You can pay people to do everything that you don't enjoy. You write your own job description, as well as everyone else's. No one is crazy enough to write a job description for a job they wouldn't want to do! (Are they?)

If you are smiling right now, it is because you know what it *really* takes to start and build something that delivers such a level of freedom. It can take years to get there, and it is seldom an easy road. Many entrepreneurs never make it that far.

But it *could* be true. The idealized vision people have of a business owner's life is not wrong, although it may often be premature. The entrepreneur always believes that such a lifestyle exists in the future, although he hasn't gotten there yet. It will take a lot of work, a lot of talent, and at least a modicum of luck to make it happen, but he is sure that it *will* happen.

It *should* be true, but along the way too many entrepreneurs become bogged down in the "lots of hard work for inadequate reward" stage of building a business. As their businesses grow, they are drawn away from what they enjoyed the most, from what they do best, and into what the business *demands* that they do. They become farmers.

Running a business should be fun. It should be rewarding. It should be something you look forward to every day and which thrills you every hour that you are there. It should fan the flames of your passion, not swallow them. It should send you home at night relaxed and happy about what you've done, not merely worried about what you didn't do.

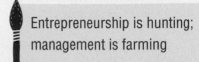

Entrepreneurship is hunting; management is farming

Your job is to hunt. For thousands of years, hunters brought in the food. Other people skinned it and cooked it. You can be certain of one thing: *there would not be more to eat if the hunters were busy skinning and cooking.* That is why there are so few entrepreneurs, and so many folks employed by them.

As an entrepreneur, you owe it to your company, your employees, your customers, and yourself to avoid getting tied down in farming activities. You started your business to do what you do best—not so that you could teach yourself a set of skills that you had little inclination to learn in the first place.

The Entrepreneurial Relationship

Entrepreneurs and their lifestyles can't be understood well by those who have worked their entire lives focused on a regular paycheck. Wage earners often compare building a business to building a house. That comparison does not even begin to come close to describing the all-consuming commitment of an entrepreneur who grows an organization from scratch.

If building a company were like building a house, it would be a house that you designed, from choosing the building site to the appearance of every stick of furniture in it. You would pick out each board and each brick individually. You would design the rooms and place every door and window exactly where you wanted it. You would teach the tradesmen how to hammer nails and spread mortar in the way that you prefer. Everything about the house would reflect your personal taste and preferences.

That is what the connection to your own business is like. You determine the business model, the products or services, and the method of delivery. You hire each person, at least in the beginning, and teach each of them exactly how you want things done in your company. Your representation to the rest of the world, your logo, motto, marketing materials, and packaging are an expression of your experience and beliefs.

Can you imagine starting a business where you first hire a business architect to determine what your business model should be? Then you would hire a business engineer to decide how to build it and a business designer to choose the appearance for you. For most entrepreneurs that wouldn't be a business; it would be a job. Building a business is *nothing* like building a home. It's much more.

The Farming Trap

Scores of entrepreneurs have told me, "This was so much more fun when it was just me and a couple of employees." A few of those also say that they made more money as a startup than as a bigger organization.

Many entrepreneurs fall into the trap of outworking everyone around them, performing the day-to-day chores of operating the business. Their work ethic, their focus on defining a target and hitting it, is what made most business owners successful in the first place.

Having taught every employee his or her job, they don't trust anyone else to teach them how to do it right. Because cash is scarce, they try to control every decision that affects profitability. They hover over estimates and bids. They personally approve all expenses. In an attempt to control *everything*, they take on farming tasks that steal time from being an entrepreneur.

As the business grows, they add to their own workload first. Entrepreneurs are impatient with others, resentful of the time it takes their less creative employees to figure out a problem, or for the less ambitious to implement a solution. They drift away from the focus on hunting that first built the business

> Hunters who attempt to control every task become farmers

and spend ever-increasing hours on the farming chores of keeping it going.

The business stops growing, but the owner's workload does not. He or she becomes frustrated because working harder doesn't produce the results that it once did. The owner is contributing all he knows, all that he can think of, into the company with insufficient results. It is not much fun anymore.

To succeed as a hunter, you have to define your role in your business. You must focus on the things that you should be doing, and stop doing the things that drain your energy. You have to make your company into something that you want to build and grow every day.

Doing what you are best at is your role in your business. Humankind first figured out job descriptions about 10,000 years ago. The first social structure, the tribe, was successful because it allowed people to focus on what they did best. Hunters should hunt.

How did you start out in your business? Were you previously employed in your field? Did you inherit your business, buy your business, or start your business from 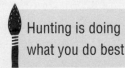 scratch? Perhaps your business is still an idea, and you are reading this book for a better approach to developing it successfully.

Hunting is doing what you do best

If you started your company from scratch, or bought it from another owner, the odds are good that you have the hunter's gene. If you inherited your business from a family member, or purchased your former place of employment after years of being an employee, you may or may not meet the normal definition of an entrepreneur, but you still need to develop the skills of a hunter in order to thrive.

Throughout this book, we will refer to entrepreneurs and business owners interchangeably. I presume that you want to make your business more successful or else you would not have read this far. Hunting is the core entrepreneurial skill. No one ever grew a company, much less a highly successful company, by being a better bookkeeper than his competitors. (Unless of course, your business is selling and delivering bookkeeping services!)

We talk about entrepreneurs in the context of business ownership because it is easily understood as a frame of reference. If you are an employed entrepreneur, someone who earns a living from your ability to find your own opportunities, and whose compensation depends solely on your ability to hunt, then everything that we discuss will apply to you as well.

Chapter 2
"I'm a little bit ADD."

HAVE A FRIEND who attended college with me in New Jersey. He was much more studious than I was and went to medical school. As a physician, he specialized in psychiatry. Eventually, he taught a class in Adult Attention Deficit Disorder at Johns Hopkins Medical School.

One day, we were having lunch and I said, "You know Andy, I sometimes think that I might have ADD." He laughed. "John," he said, "When I teach my class I have your picture mentally in front of me."

Many of a hunter's behavioral strengths are diagnosed as "problems," because they do not fit easily in the farmers' world. I've found that those same traits can be channeled into great results, if you recognize them and use them properly.

Farmer Prejudice

Before any business owner can join one of our peer advisory boards, I conduct a ninety-minute interview. Among the key questions that I ask are "What is your greatest strength? What makes you *good* at running your business?"

I have heard one answer so many times that I can recognize the body language even before the words are spoken. The interviewee seems to shrink a little bit in the chair. His eyes may look away. His posture and voice change into what I think of as "confession" mode.

"First, you have to understand ... I think I'm a little bit ADD."

Then they begin their defense. "Not that I've been diagnosed, of course. I don't take medication or anything. I just seem to have a problem focusing on the things that I should be focused on."

Well, I *have* been diagnosed by an expert in the field. Attention Deficit Disorder is a label put on hunters by farmers. It is their way of saying that hunters are less able to compete in a society where farming skills dominate. They are wrong. Hunters are the best competitors, honed by eons of natural selection.

In 1997, Thom Hartmann wrote *Attention Deficit Disorder, A Different Perception.* It quickly became known as the "Hunter and Farmer Book." I owe my original realization of the link between entrepreneurs and hunters to Mr. Hartmann's insights.

It isn't that all entrepreneurs are ADD, although with the massive over-diagnosis of that "condition," most might be labeled as such using current standards. Hartmann argues that ADD children are displaying characteristics that were not only acceptable, but also desirable and prized in earlier times. I believe that entrepreneurs are displaying traits necessary both for success in private business and for the survival of our society as a whole.

The problem is not that there is something *wrong* with these traits; it's that the common wisdom of how to utilize those skills is erroneous. In a world of farmers, the hunter is an oddity. He stands out. We are always suspicious of those who stand out when they are supposed to blend in.

I will discuss the pervasiveness of farming mentality in the next chapter, but for now, it is sufficient to say that farming is all about doing things systematically. A huge portion of common business knowledge tells entrepreneur hunters that they have to become farmers in order to succeed.

- Manage what you measure.
- Develop job descriptions.
- Know your numbers.
- Pursue Six Sigma quality.
- Failure to plan is planning to fail.

- Achieve ISO 9000 certification.
- Document your policies and procedures.
- Runaway growth is dangerous.
- The devil is in the details.

Where are the words that appeal to the hunters?

- Do something you love.
- Make a lot of money.
- Don't sweat the small stuff.
- Work hard.
- Have fun.

Which one gets you more excited, the first collection of "business knowledge" or the second list? If you chose the second, you might be ADD but at the very least, you have the makings of a hunter.

Look at the traits of a typical ADD "sufferer":

Overly distracted, frequently late, forgetful, overwhelmed by responsibilities, a dreamer, a tendency to overlook details, poor listening skills, hyperactive focus for long periods on a single task, a tendency to procrastinate, underestimating the time needed to complete tasks, relationship problems stemming from a tendency to tune out things that interfere with what they are doing. (Helpguide.org: *Adult ADD/ADHD, signs symptoms, effects and treatment*)

Dang, that is a description of 90% of the business owners I know. We should replace that with the *hunter's diagnosis:*

Works tirelessly in pursuit of a vision not seen by others, juggles more responsibilities than normal people can handle, able to get the big picture, sees the potential outcome of actions through multiple iterations and decision trees, carries the burden of providing not only for his own family, but for the families of those who work for him, accepts the liability of bad results as a consequence of making decisions, accomplishes massive amounts of work while understanding that he will never, ever be "caught up," functions in chaos when everyone else is panicking, has no time to waste listening to idiots, can accomplish huge projects in short time frames, able to leap mid-sized buildings with a running start.

There you have it. The hunter's diagnosis doesn't contradict the ADD diagnosis. In fact, many of the behaviors described are identical. It is just a different perspective. What the farmers think of as a problem, hunters should recognize as ability.

Look back at the prologue. What were the traits of our Hunter of 7,000 years ago? He solved problems. He developed alternate solutions. He organized other people to be more effective. He recognized and used talent where it could do the most good. He ignored personal pain and deprivation. He stayed laser-focused on the task for extended periods. He took responsibility for the well-being of others. People did what he told them to do.

In a later age, our prehistoric hunter would have been a terrific entrepreneur.

Typically, when a business owner gives me the answer, "I'm a little bit ADD," he follows with "You see, I like building new things. Once it becomes routine, I have difficulty paying attention to it. I kind of lose interest."

Of course he does. The hunter hunted. Once he brought in the game, the rest of the tribe was responsible for the skinning and cooking. As humans perfected agriculture, the roles began to change. The other members of the tribe had previously spent their time either waiting for the hunters to bring something home, or else working on the last carcass the hunters provided. With the advent of agriculture, the whole tribe worked all day tilling and watering the crops. They were understandably less inclined to work all evening while the hunters sat around the fire swapping hunting stories.

Hunting by itself was no longer enough. The hunters had to pitch in with other chores. Crops provided a more dependable food supply and required constant attention. However, when the crops failed, there was only the hunter to fall back on. When times were good, the hunter provided protein. As humans learned to domesticate animals, even that need was fulfilled by people who could easily be taught the necessary skills.

We lionize the leaders of large corporations in the media; the Jack Welch or Steve Jobs type of charismatic leader with billions of dollars and tens of thousands of employees at his command. These leaders are profiled as examples to be emulated. The media portrays them as risk takers and gamblers who will "bet the bank" on a new idea or market.

The vast majority of leaders in large organizations spend their entire working lives in large organizations. They have never missed a paycheck. If they Hunters have no guarantees against failure fail, it is a failure to meet a budget, or failure to reach a sales goal. It isn't a failure to provide for their family. In the case of the most extreme failures, they are fired. Often, that comes with a severance package of a few years' salary and benefits. Sometimes, it comes with a golden parachute sufficient to provide a comfortable lifestyle for them and their descendants for generations.

Entrepreneurs don't have contracts guaranteeing anything if they fail. They have no golden parachute, and usually have no parachute at all. Many small businesses owe their success to one man or woman who overcame challenges on the adrenalin of sheer terror. They knew that if they failed, the dark abyss of starvation (or at least deprivation) faced their families.

In the prehistoric tribe, the hunter's role was deemphasized over centuries in favor of agriculture and animal husbandry. In modern business, the entrepreneur's role has been deemphasized in favor of those who manage complex enterprises and financial structures.

However, when the crops failed, the tribe quickly turned back to the hunter to provide for them. Thousands of years later, in the Great Recession of 2009, the business press and politicians looked to small business as the engine that would save the economy. All the complex derivatives, all the mergers and acquisitions, suddenly shrank in importance when the economy needed someone to hunt, to come up with new ideas and to create new jobs. Society still needs hunters to hunt.

Maybe they should stop criticizing the characteristics that make it possible.

A LIfetime of Working with Hunters

Why should I be the one to write this book? More importantly, why should you read it? I am not a multi-millionaire, although I have managed to make a decent income while signing my own paychecks for over thirty years. I have never owned a business that made Inc. Magazine's top 500 list, although I've worked with several that did. However, I do possess a unique knowledge of what makes a successful hunter.

In the last fifteen years, I have worked exclusively with the owners of over 400 companies as their consultant and coach. They have revenues ranging from $300,000 to $450,000,000 annually, and employ anywhere from three to 1,500 employees in manufacturing, distribution, retailing, food service, oil and gas, professional services, construction, health care, technology, automotive, and transportation. They are male and female and range in age from their mid-twenties to their late seventies.

As of this writing, we have spent nearly 11,000 hours together in face-to-face coaching, consulting, peer group meetings, and interviews. That is 11,000 hours of listening to business owners solve problems, test theories, trade experiences and float new ideas. As one long meeting, it would consume eight hours a day, Monday through Friday, for five years without vacations or holidays.

Boredom is never an issue. We spend our one-on-one coaching sessions discussing an owner's hopes and ambitions, and focusing on building new value or pursuing new opportunities. Each new client brings fresh experience and ideas into the conversation. My knowledge base of business problems and their solutions grows daily. I also understand entrepreneurship on a more visceral level. Before I advised owners about running companies, I had several of my own.

As a kid growing up in the Ramapo Mountains of northern New Jersey, I was always the top seller of candy bars and greeting cards for my school. I had lemonade stands and created carnivals in my backyard, which I promoted well enough that the neighborhood kids begged their mothers for spare change for the "rides."

After dropping out of college (I finished later), I got a job on the loading dock with a warehouse distributor, where I detailed cars for other employees on my lunch break. Not surprisingly, I transferred to a job in sales and became the top salesperson. Eventually, my employers offered me a partnership in their failing California operation if I could turn it around. I was thirty years old and my first lesson in business ownership was a harsh one, but more about that in a moment.

Since then, I have owned a manufacturing company, a healthcare management company, and two consulting firms. The current fashionable term for this kind of career path is "serial entrepreneur," but I sometimes think that "chronically unemployable" might be a better description.

The Light Bulb

In California, we assembled a new sales team (the incumbents had all been fired) and grew the branch's revenue from $1 million to over $5 million in fifteen months. I was acting as a salesperson and running the warehouse while supervising the construction of a new facility, hiring new employees, purchasing inventory and managing day-to-day operations. I had no management training (my degree is in accounting) and I kept doing every critical job and making every important decision personally.

Mr. Handreke was the senior partner of the German company that had purchased a minority position in our business. When our margins began to slide, he came to California for a visit. He told me plainly that the declining profits made it appear that I was not up to the job.

I protested, of course. Not only had I engineered amazing results in sales, but I was working eighty or ninety hours each week. As he listed the areas where my company was underperforming, I finally exclaimed in frustration, "I practically live here. I'm always the first to arrive and the last to leave. I can't possibly work any harder!"

Mr. Handreke looked at me for a moment. "John," he said, "If you were returning record profits, do you think I would have come to California to ask why you were leaving the office early?"

I suddenly realized that I had become a farmer. A very hard working farmer, but then most farmers work very hard. I had stopped being a hunter.

That lesson stuck with me, but I wish I could say that it changed my behavior right away. Like many hunters, I had to learn it more than once. The German partners eventually bought out all the other owners, and put one of their own people in to run the company. I took on a few more business turnarounds, and then drifted into consulting. Like many folks, consulting to me was something to do between "real" jobs. In my case, it has been covering the gap in my employment for over twenty years.

When I worked in California, I belonged to an executive peer group called Adaptive Business Leaders, run by my friend Mimi Grant. It was a great experience and my group helped me through many business issues. I eventually moved to San Antonio to allow more time with my family while traveling nationally for my consulting practice. Even from a more central location, my travel was almost constant. I thought that running a peer organization would be an ideal way to meet other business owners and to find local business opportunities. I began developing a plan to create a peer group organization in Texas.

Stuck in First Class on the runway at LaGuardia airport during the winter of 1997, I was on my second cocktail (I do miss all those consultant's frequent flyer miles!) when I saw an ad for an "executive's dream franchise." I called the number, and found The Alternative Board® (TAB), a franchisor that helps consultants learn to coach business owners and facilitate peer advisory groups.

I purchased the franchise without even visiting TAB's offices. I was a fully developed hunter and I understood what my strengths were. I didn't need anyone to teach me how to sell my services or deliver them, but I recognized that developing systems wasn't what I did well. Within eighteen months, I was the most successful franchise in TAB's history by number of clients, and held that title until I sold half of my territory in 2010.

That is how I accumulated 11,000 hours of face-to-face consulting and coaching. This book contains the combined experience of hundreds of successful entrepreneurs. I'm just one of them; one who has been lucky enough to listen to and collect their knowledge. This book is about what they know.

Chapter 3
Types of Hunters

TO PARAPHRASE WILLIAM SHAKESPEARE, some people are born hunters, some achieve huntership, and some become hunters because it is thrust upon them.

In Michael Gerber's book *The E-Myth*, the "myth" is that entrepreneurs are usually visionary individuals who assemble labor and capital to create wealth. In reality, Gerber says, most small business owners are people formerly employed doing something for someone else, who then began doing it for themselves.

I agree. Most business founders cite one of two reasons for starting their companies. Many lost a job and couldn't find another, so began working for themselves. Most of the rest simply wanted to make more money than their boss was willing to pay them.

Not all small businesses are run by their founders. Those who began as self-employed Technicians usually bootstrapped, or started with little more than their own abilities. Creators fulfilled Gerber's entrepreneurial myth by taking an idea and assembling resources to implement it. Inheritors and Acquirers, however, assumed ownership of existing businesses. Technicians, Inheritors, Acquirers and Creators are the four types of business owners. However, just owning a business does not necessarily make you an entrepreneur. Each type of business owner includes both hunters and farmers in its ranks.

Owning a business does not necessarily make you an entrepreneur

Technicians

The Technician is the basic entrepreneur. He learned a job. Then he began to think, "If I know how to do this, I could do it for myself."

When the Technician goes into business, he does not have a company. Typically, he doesn't have a business plan. He has a job. By doing the actual work of revenue generation, he starts out trapped in an employee role, with one major change—he has a lousy boss. Now he can't ask for a day off because there is no one else to do the job. He goes to work when he is sick. He makes excuses to his family for missing events. He takes on difficult or marginal customers because he cannot afford to pass up any revenue opportunity.

Most start-up small business owners started out as Technicians. Frequently, their initial research was no more than looking at their paycheck, and then looking at what their employer charged for their work. "Why, I am getting less than *half* of what they collect for my efforts! I could do the same work and keep *all* of the money!"

Perhaps that plan actually works for a little while. They avoid "unnecessary" expenses, like liability insurance or legal incorporation. They drive their personal vehicles for work ("Hey, it's tax deductible!"). They use personal cell phones as the business number. They establish a corporate office in the bedroom ("Hey, it's tax deductible!").

In a short time, the Technician begins to see where his former employer's enviable margins went. His personal contacts in the business aren't sufficient to keep him busy all the time. He has to figure out some way to tell people what he does, so adds marketing expenses to his overhead. He builds a basic website and sends out some direct mail. He grows tired of his personal cell phone ringing at 1 o'clock in the morning with customer questions, so he gets a separate phone number for the business.

The Technician comes home after a long day to a bunch of voice messages or emails that he no longer has the time to return. He decides to get an answering service or hire a virtual assistant. His vehicle begins to break down under the additional load of both work and family needs. He begins to appreciate how much it really costs to keep him out doing the work of the business.

Finally, he lands more work than he can handle personally. It is time to choose between limiting his income and hiring an employee to do some of the work for him. For many Technician start-ups, it doesn't go

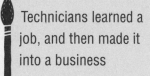

Technicians learned a job, and then made it into a business

much further. They limit their future with their first major decision—to do only what they can do themselves.

According to the U.S. Small Business Administration, about 17,000,000 of the 26,000,000 small businesses in the United States have either zero or one employee. Those are mostly the self-employed Technicians who never made it beyond having a job. They are not entrepreneurs, nor are they hunters. They are simply farmers who grow only enough to feed themselves. Within five years of starting up, about 85% of them will give up and return to the employed workforce.

However, some Technicians have the hunter gene. They come to the realization that they can't grow a real business if they are personally doing the work all day. The leap of faith It took to go out on their own is miniscule compared to the next leap of faith, hiring someone else to do the work. They have started to build a company, and assumed the responsibility of providing for more than just their immediate family. They become hunters.

The transition from self-employed to employer can be a scary experience. For the first time, a Technician is deliberately taking on more than he can personally handle. He accepts responsibility for the quality of work that isn't his own. He is suddenly in the middle, between an employee who depends on him for an income and a customer who trusts him to deliver as promised.

There is no guidebook for making the leap of faith from the ranks of the self-employed into those of people who build companies. I don't think it can be taught. You either believe that you can continue to generate more work than one person can handle or you don't. You are either a hunter or you're not.

Inheritors

Inheritors are former employees who found themselves owning a business. The Inheritor might be a family member of the owner, but just as frequently is a long-time employee who assumed ownership from a retiring founder.

Inheritors developed in a system. The founder of the company, whom the law of averages says was probably a Technician, created processes that were at least good enough to sustain the business, and may have been good enough to grow a very successful enterprise.

The physicians' Hippocratic Oath is commonly thought to begin with the phrase "First, do no harm." (It is a misquote, and that phrase is actually not in the oath.) However, for many Inheritors, especially second-generation owners, it could be considered their management oath. They assumed control of a working machine. They were taught by a boss or a parent (perhaps the same person) to operate it in a certain way. Unless there is a malfunction, they are expected to keep the machine running as it always has.

Inheritors do not have the, "It's all mine; I built it myself." attachment to the business. If an Inheritor was originally hired by the founder, he was taught to do everything the way the founder wanted it done. If they are the children of the founder, they were raised in a culture where "look at what I built for you" was mentioned regularly. In either case, the Inheritor is trained to maintain the system; to keep thing running the same.

Unfortunately, "The best laid plans of mice and men often go astray..." (That is a quote, from Robert Burns). Companies change. Employees change. Products change. Industries change. Markets change. The biggest challenge for Inheritors is understanding when the working machine needs an overhaul to keep functioning successfully.

Many, and perhaps most Inheritors are farmers. They perceive change as undesirable, and can become overly dependent on the existing systems working under any circumstances. They may have never had the hunting instincts of the founder, or may have suppressed them. When faced with changing circumstances, their first defense is to try to return things to the way they were before.

Family successions are especially difficult. Only about one-third of successful family businesses survive the transition through a second generation of ownership. Experience does not make the subsequent success rate any better. Two-thirds of those under the second generation of ownership fail to make it to a third, and three-fourths of those who enter a third generation get no further. The combined odds of even a *successful* family business being run by a fourth generation of family are about three out of every hundred. (Joseph Astrachan, PhD, editor, Family Business Review)

When I develop a client's exit plan for internal succession, the financial aspects of the founder's retirement are only half of the equation. The other half concentrates on transferring the responsibilities and hunter's perspective of the original owners to new owners. Just teaching them the managerial skills to maintain daily operations is not sufficient.

You cannot keep a company running the same way forever, whether it is making buggy whips or computers. In their time, companies that produced wooden ladders, multi-volume encyclopedias, and do-it-yourself electronics kits all appeared to have a steady and dependable market niche. All are now out of business. **Inheritors assumed control of a working machine**

An Inheritor may be a farmer, but he seldom can stay that way and also expand the business. Inheritors who can develop beyond managing the systems they were originally taught have companies that grow and thrive. Those who cannot change become another one of the vast majority who fall by the wayside.

Some Inheritors are natural hunters. Some are farmers who learn to be hunters. The rest remain in business until it exceeds their experience.

Acquirers

Acquirers are business owners who purchased their businesses. They bought an existing business from another entrepreneur. These owners are almost inevitably hunters.

In my years of acting as an intermediary in the sale of businesses, I have come to understand that there is one overwhelming influence on a business buyer's decision. He has to believe that he can run a better business than the previous owner. Just as importantly, the Acquirer doesn't want to reinvent the wheel, or be bogged down in developing basic processes and systems. He wants something that is working already, so that he can focus on making it bigger. That is clearly a hunter's mentality.

There is a subset of Acquirers whose motivations are not as clear-cut. These buyers want a proven opportunity and they aren't particularly interested in changing it. They are the buyers who acquire franchises.

> **Acquirers believe that they can run a business better than the current owner**

Franchising began in the 1920s, but was originally limited to selling products. Early franchise pioneers, including Coca-Cola and the Singer Sewing Company, sold a geographic sales territory and the exclusive right to represent their product. In the case of Coca-Cola, for example, that included bottling the beverage locally to save on transportation costs, but the "secret formula" syrup was purchased from the franchisor.

In the mid-1940s a new kind of franchise was created, the *Business Model Franchise*. Begun by industry pioneers like Howard Johnson, Roy Allen and Frank Wright (A&W Root Beer), and Harland Sanders at Kentucky Fried Chicken, these franchises offered a comprehensive system for running a company that required little or no prior business knowledge to be successful. They were the first turnkey businesses.

Business model franchises were first sold to returning World War II GIs who wanted to be in business for themselves. There were 200 new franchises sold in 1950, 700 in 1960 and 2,000 in 1970. Franchising really took off, however, when a generation of post-war Baby Boomers began looking for career success. Crowded out of corporate America by their sheer numbers, the Boomers bought franchises with breathtaking speed. In 1975, the first Boomers started to turn thirty years old, and the number of franchises sold annually jumped from 2,000 to an astonishing *22,000 per year* in the five years from 1976 to 1980.

Many Boomer franchisees bought their businesses because they needed a job. They wanted the security of a tested system. Some of the challenges of running a business, such as marketing and advertising, would be handled by the franchisor. The franchisee started with a detailed procedure manual describing how to execute every task in the business. Those Acquirers are farmers, and for them, franchising had much more in common with employment than with entrepreneurship.

Some franchisees bought their businesses for quite different reasons. They knew that they were not suited to developing procedures. They had little interest in figuring out how to do the work of the business. They wanted to run businesses and saw a franchise as the fastest and easiest way to get there. They came into the franchise system expecting to be successful enough to grow rapidly and focused on growth, leaving the development of management systems to the franchisor. Some of those Acquirers wound up owning hundreds of businesses within the system, and a few actually wound up owning the entire franchise system.

They are the hunter franchisees. They saw the management infrastructure of a franchise as an opportunity to focus on doing what they did best: hunt.

The sheer number of farmer-franchisees who purchase jobs dwarfs the Acquirers who seek to buy freestanding small businesses. Those business owners don't have the flexibility of making it up as they go. When we talk about Acquirers, we are referring to those who purchased a business with a hunter's intention of changing and improving it.

Creators

Creators are the entrepreneur's entrepreneurs. They began their businesses as a business, not merely as a way to make a living. They hunted from the outset; for investment capital, resources, talent, and markets.

Creators are not only disinterested in doing the work of the business; they may carefully avoid even learning how the work is done. They have an idea, and assemble capital and resources with the specific objective of creating wealth. It is the purist's definition of entrepreneurship.

Even Creators can slide into farming. As the company grows, they may become overwhelmed by the number of balls that have to be kept in the air. A key employee may leave, dragging the Creator into the role of a manager or even that of a Technician. Changing economic or market conditions can cripple performance, and the Creator may respond like an Inheritor, with a single-minded focus on keeping their original great idea alive.

> Creators are the purist's definition of entrepreneurship

Most Creators can outlast a downturn, because they are inventive enough to develop new ideas and strategies. Those who cannot, because either they are fixated on their initial concept, or because they can't attract the talent they need to transform their ideas into reality, often slip into stagnation—a farming failure.

The first step toward hunting in a world of farmers is to determine which type of owner you are, and more importantly, which type you would like to be.

Chapter 4
What Makes a Hunter?

EVERY BUSINESS OWNER SHOULD RECOGNIZE him or herself in at least one and perhaps several, of the previous profiles. If you aren't an owner, the observations in this book are also applicable to anyone who wants to be successful as a hunter in business.

Not all successful business owners are hunters. Some owners build or assume companies with well-developed systems and processes, and refine those incrementally for greater success. Similarly, most employees are farmers, but plenty of employee-hunters are vital contributors in organizations that can recognize and utilize them properly. Your family commitments may not afford the flexibility to take business risks right now, or you may not be interested in managing other people. That does not necessarily make you a farmer.

We see examples of non-owner hunters every day. Salespeople, at least the top professionals, are hunters who choose to leave the details of anything but sales to others. Other hunters may be project, division or branch managers. In fact, most jobs that compensate based on performance, especially those where a material portion of the compensation is based on profitability, are attractive to hunters.

Not everyone has the opportunity to go into business. Life happens along the way. An early marriage, children, a sick parent, or any of a thousand other things can derail your intentions. That doesn't mean you have to become a farmer. (Remember, farmers make sure we can still eat when the hunters are unsuccessful.)

But, if you want to be a successful hunter, you will need to master three traits. They are ubiquitous in all hunters, and are prerequisites for successful entrepreneurship.

The First Trait: Creativity

Hunters solve problems. They look at every situation as a puzzle that has an answer. It may not be an obvious answer, and it may not be the answer they want, but they fervently believe that there is an answer. Failure merely means that they haven't found the *right* answer yet.

Jeff Salter is the CEO and majority shareholder of Caring Senior Service. CSS provides in-home nonmedical care for those who, due to age or disability, cannot care for themselves. Every day, thousands of CSS caregivers across the USA go into people's homes to help them cook, clean, and bathe. Sometimes, they are simply companions for the lonely.

Jeff was working his way through college as a customer service representative for a home health agency in Midland, Texas. He noticed a large number of requests for help with Activities of Daily Living (ADLs). The home health agency that he worked for was limited to nursing care and medically related services.

Jeff's first solution was to locate a provider that could help his clients. He would happily refer them to another company, if that would solve his customer's problem, but no such services were available in Midland.

Jeff quit his job to open Caring Senior Service. In a very short time, the business became so busy that he had to quit college as well. Jeff had identified a problem and solved it. People needed his services.

Soon, Jeff opened a second office in McAllen, Texas, then another in Corpus Christi. San Antonio followed, then Austin. In five years, Jeff had quickly built a substantial company with over 200 employees.

Success brought a new set of problems. The growth of CSS was limited only by its infrastructure. Jeff did not have enough experience on his management team to open new offices as fast as the market demanded, so he decided to franchise. Working with franchise business owners, he reasoned, would relieve his team from having to manage each individual office. He could focus on a plan for opening more company-owned offices parallel with new franchise locations.

Some of the franchisees were very successful, but others were not. Feeling an obligation to the people who contracted with CSS franchises for care, Jeff repurchased the failing franchises and converted them to company locations.

However, those offices were far away. They weren't in markets that had been planned by CSS; rather, they were wherever a prospective franchisee had thought they might be successful. The infrastructure requirements of handling these far-flung locations expanded by the day and the company, once again, stalled in its growth.

Jeff came up with a new solution. He would find experienced operators with track records of success. Local owners of small in-home service companies could be joint venture partners with CSS. They could combine with the CSS offices in an area. The combined company would have experienced management, the CSS national support and software capabilities, and economies of scale in operations. The small agency owners would have access to CSS systems, fewer details to worry about, and greater profitability.

CSS entered into several joint ventures and Jeff handed off his company offices in those areas. Then he recognized another problem. There was a reason that small agency owners were small. Most lacked either the skills, or the desire to be bigger. They couldn't surrender the details to someone else. They did not like managing multiple locations. They did a lot of the work in their own office personally, and abdicated rather than delegated responsibility in their branch locations. Again, the company's growth slowed to a crawl.

Jeff was not starving. CSS was already large enough to provide him with an excellent living; but he wanted the company to be a lot more than it was. He saw the failure of the joint ventures as merely another problem to solve.

He reorganized CSS again, dissolving the joint ventures, either by dividing the offices into freestanding sites or selling them off to his joint venture partners. He closed some of the reclaimed branches and several of the company-run franchises as well. He erased his organizational chart, and recreated CSS as a pure franchisor with all functions focused on supporting franchisees. He changed the status of his original company stores from corporate to simply the holdings of the largest single franchisee, himself.

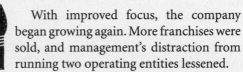

Hunters don't defend failing solutions

With improved focus, the company began growing again. More franchises were sold, and management's distraction from running two operating entities lessened.

Did Jeff solve the problem? He would be the first to say, "For now." He understands that CSS' renewed growth will again bring new challenges and the need for new solutions.

Hunters don't defend their failing solutions. In fact, they are usually the first to see that they are not working. Often, they develop a new answer before others even notice there is a problem. Sometimes, they develop answers to things that aren't even problems yet.

That doesn't mean that hunters are exceptional planners. Often, they are just the opposite. They may not have a Plan B and a Plan C when they begin Plan A. Alternatives would only distract them from a total focus on making Plan A work. However, if Plan A fails they will develop Plan B and pursue it with the same single-mindedness that they recently devoted to Plan A.

Hunters believe that there is a solution to every problem, and that the only things they need are the time and resources to figure it out. "I can't possibly do that" simply isn't in their vocabulary. They will keep trying until they find a way.

The Second Trait: Tenacity

Some entrepreneurs are incredibly lucky. They have a new idea; they start a business, and the money rolls in. All they have left to do is count it. If that is your expectation, I am afraid you are in for a disappointment. Some businesses succeed because they were in exactly the right place at exactly the right time, but those represent a small minority.

I have asked hundreds of business owners whom they would rather have for a partner, someone who was very, very talented, or someone who was just very, very lucky. Every last one of them picks the lucky partner each and every time. Not one experienced business owner has ever opted for talent over luck. They know that some luck is required to succeed, and that a lot of luck is better than a lot of skill.

I will assume you are among the other 99.99% of us—the ones who have to make it happen. For people like us, things don't always work on the first try. Sometimes things don't work on the twenty-first try. In fact, I've met many business owners whose companies *should* have failed. They were not a great idea to start with, and the founder lacked the business skills to develop the idea properly. Through sheer tenacity, those owners managed to keep a business alive until they learned how to make it successful.

Lara August owns Robot Creative, an award-winning design firm. Like many creative businesses, Robot started out with one person— the owner. As time passed, Lara began adding employees to work on design under her supervision.

Robot Creative grew, and Lara's overhead grew with it. She joined a business owners' peer group (one of mine in The Alternative Board®) to combine her brainpower with that of other small business owners.

One morning, Lara was very quiet in our monthly meeting. When her turn came to discuss business, she was nearly in tears. "I'm afraid this will be my last meeting," she told her group. "My office rent is due Friday and I can't pay it. We've gone two months without landing a new project. I have just enough in the bank to make the next payroll and then we are done. I don't know what will happen when I can't pay my rent. Will I be kicked out? Will they lock the doors and take my equipment?"

The other members started laughing, which was *certainly* not the kind of supportive reaction that Lara expected. Then they went around the table, one by one.

"Why, I once had to pay my rent in services for almost a year. The landlord wasn't happy, but he could use my services more than he could use the empty space."

"I had to give up my office and forwarded the phone number to my home for a few months. I had voicemail put on it. 'For accounting, dial 1, for sales, dial 2, for customer service, dial 3.' It didn't matter what you dialed, it rang on the phone in my kitchen."

"You aren't broke. Broke is when you have taken the last of the family's savings out of the bank to pay company bills and you don't dare tell your spouse."

"That's nothing. It is when you take the last of your savings, put it in the company checking account, cut yourself a paycheck, then go home to show the check to your wife as evidence that the business is finally becoming successful. That's when you *know* you have to come through!"

Hunters don't recognize defeat

Lara realized that she wasn't the first to face the dark abyss of business oblivion. She took the group's advice on negotiating with her landlord, increased the pressure on her employees to help her hunt for work, and the business survived. Robot Creative continues to win awards and wow clients today, more than ten years later.

The stories from Lara's peer group remind me of a t-shirt my son wore as a high school wrestler. You've probably seen the cartoon before. A crane is swallowing a frog. All that is visible of the frog are his back legs and one front leg stretching out from the crane's beak down to its throat, which the frog is clenching tightly to prevent the crane's swallow from being completed. The caption is, "Never quit!"

Hunters never quit. There are no defeats, only setbacks. In the toughest times, they still focus on the next sale, the next problem, the next deal. Success is just a little further down the road.

These two traits, creativity and tenacity, combine to form the core of a hunter's personality—indefatigable problem solving. "No" is never the answer and "Never" is not an option.

Of course, these two characteristics aren't *everything* you need to build a successful business. They are just the indispensable building blocks, the foundation for all that follows. How you put them to work will determine your long-term result.

These two traits come together often. Let's call it tenacious creativity. When faced with challenges, entrepreneurs think of solutions. If the solution doesn't work, they think of another, then another and another. That tenacious approach to serial creativity is often how they survive long enough to become successful.

The Third Eye

I was coaching with my friend and client, Steve O'Donnell of Hill Country Bakery, when he offered a third required trait. He called it "the ability to navigate in the fog." I thought, "What a great way to phrase it!" (Moreover, like any good consultant, I immediately appropriated it for my own use.)

Some folks call it vision, but the hunter's third eye is more than just knowing where you want your business to go. It is knowing how to keep moving in the right direction when you don't have a compass and there aren't any signposts. It is innately comprehending what will get you closer to your goals and what will distract you from them. The third eye of entrepreneurship is a sixth sense for when to listen to advice from others and when to ignore it. It's having a sense of direction in your gut that lets you instinctively choose the right path.

Many religions have the third eye concept. It appears in Taoism, Hinduism, Confucianism and Gnostic Christianity. It refers to an instinctive knowledge that cannot be explained by the usual five senses.

> Hunters know when to listen to others and when to ignore them

It may be clairvoyance, or psychic vision, or foretelling the future. It may be all of those things. In an entrepreneur, the third eye is often referred to as a "gut feeling."

Entrepreneurs hire the person who may not best fit the qualifications, but who has some experience that shows the right attitude. They take on the customer whom their competitors consider too demanding, in the belief that their company can raise its game to the level necessary. They sell the job that is too big for them to handle, with the confidence that they will deliver as promised, somehow.

Chaz Neely owns a wholesale supplier of steel products. An Acquirer, for over a decade he was very successful in building his company into a regional powerhouse in its industry. The profits had permitted Chaz to spend a seven-figure amount on a large home in the most expensive gated community in the city.

Then came the Savings and Loan crash of the late 80s. Chaz' customers didn't just stop buying; they disappeared. Business after business went bust, often leaving Chaz with uncollectable receivables. Soon, he wasn't paying his suppliers and his own business was in danger of bankruptcy.

Chaz went home one night and told his wife that they would have to sell the house and move into an apartment. Every penny of the proceeds would need to be pumped into the company if he was going to save it.

As radio icon Paul Harvey used to say, "and now for the rest of the story." Chaz pulled the company through the recession. He was positioned to move forward as the industry strengthened, returning to rapid growth and even greater profitability. Within a few years, he had returned to the same exclusive neighborhood and bought an even bigger home.

Chaz then saw an opportunity to make a big leap in his company's growth. Adding a new line and expanding his territory promised to create a quantum leap in profitability. Unfortunately, his already smoking growth rate was stretching the company's cash flow. He was going to have to go to the bank for more working capital.

Chaz had asked the bank for help during the hard times and had, of course, been denied. This time was different. His balance sheet was stronger, sales were increasing by leaps and bounds, and margins were excellent. What was there not to like?

To his surprise, Chaz' banker turned him down flat. "We think that you are growing quite fast enough," the banker told him. "Trying to do more might stretch your business beyond your capabilities."

Chaz went home and made an announcement. "Honey, we have to sell the house again!"

Now *that* is an entrepreneur. Chaz went on to great success that continues today. He was listed in the Inc. 500 every year for over a decade, and received Ernst & Young's Entrepreneur of the Year award.

Not all of us have Chaz Neely's appetite for risk. Chaz had a vision for his business. His banker gave him sound advice; outgrowing your cash flow can be a fatal problem for a company. Chad knew where he wanted to go, however, and he wouldn't let anything get in his way.

Every entrepreneur has a vision for his or her company. For some, it is enshrined in a vision statement. Unfortunately, those often become bogged down in an attempt to mention all the right required factors. Too many vision statements sound like this; *"We will be a leader in our industry, delivering outstanding products and impeccable service to our valuable customers through the efforts of our greatest asset, our irreplaceable employee team."* (Yawn.)

The vision I am discussing here is not just a statement. In fact, it may be very difficult to put into words. It is how you *feel* about your company. It is how your personality is ingrained in the company's approach to everything it does. It is communicating to every employee and vendor what you will accept in performance and what you won't. Part of the responsibility of every entrepreneur is communicating this vision in words and deeds every single day.

The third eye is clearly part of what makes a successful entrepreneur. It is more than just risk-taking. It is a confidence that your tenacious creativity will figure out a way to reach the goal. It is an unshakable belief that when confronted with possible failure, you just won't fail.

Chapter 5
Hunters aren't Perfect

IT IS POSSIBLE TO EVINCE ALL THREE TRAITS of a successful entrepreneur and still be bad at running a business. Sometimes it is just bad luck, but there are other times an entrepreneur fails because he is so good at all three traits.

A substantial part of what drives hunters is the thrill of accomplishment. There is a feeling of satisfaction in solving a problem or beating the odds. In the day-to-day repetitive tasks of running a business, these little adrenalin rushes can be the highlights. When an employee is hung up on an issue or the business faces a small crisis, it is gratifying to be the one who knows what to do.

Hunters can become addicted to that small adrenalin rush. Without realizing what they are doing, they train employees to depend on their ability to answer all the questions. They criticize actions or plans that are less effective than the ones they would have made. They enjoy being the center of all activity, even while complaining that their employees "don't know how to make a decision."

The Problem Solver's Trap

If you are the source of all decision making in your business, its growth is limited by your ongoing availability to answer questions. You become the constraining funnel for new ideas, and for solutions to the issues that arise every day. If you don't have the answer, the problem becomes unsolvable.

> Hunters can become addicted to small adrenalin rushes

A business that requires your constant attention, that stalls when you aren't there, isn't worth much. As a business broker, I know that an Acquirer is not interested in a company where he needs to know everything there is to know about the business from the first day of ownership. He expects to have some time to learn on the job. That means others, your employees and managers, should be able to make at least the small decisions, and probably the medium-risk ones as well, without intervention.

Tenacious problem solving, according to a vision of the future only you can see, is the hallmark of a successful entrepreneur. Like everything else, it is best employed in moderation. If it is the only thing that keeps a company growing, the potential for your business will be severely limited.

Surrendering Your Farmer Duties

We need to pause here for a moment to make sure that one thing is absolutely clear. Prehistoric tribes would not have grown into societies if they had relied solely on the hunters' skills. Farmers added the dependability of a steady food supply that the tribe could rely upon season after season.

Similarly, your business cannot grow and thrive to a sustainable level if it is solely dependent on your skills as a hunter. You need the farmers too. The advice of the vast majority of management books has some validity. The farming skills, management, measurement, tracking, and review really are critical to maintaining a healthy organization. They just aren't what *you* should be doing.

Many entrepreneurs misapply management advice because they confuse their leadership role with their management role. As a leader, it is your job to know where the organization is going and what you intend to accomplish. The manager's role is to steer a steady course toward those objectives. Successful entrepreneurs are far more accomplished at the skills of leadership than they are at those of management. Most small businesses would fare better if their owners focused more on their vision for the future and less on the day-to-day tasks of running the business.

In the Star Trek television shows and films, Mr. Spock is indisputably smarter than James T. Kirk. He is stronger (remember the Vulcan shoulder grip?), and he is far, far more logical. Spock constantly reminds Kirk that the probability of success for Kirk's latest plan is very low. Yet Kirk is the captain, and his plans somehow work in spite of the odds. When they fail, he just comes up with another plan (usually one with an even lower chance of succeeding).

Kirk focuses on the objective. Spock focuses on the road to the objective. Kirk is concerned with what they need to accomplish. Spock worries about how they will accomplish it. Kirk accepts setbacks and distractions. Spock regards setbacks and distractions as failures of the plan. Kirk is a leader. Spock is a manager.

Owning a business has one undeniable advantage; you can write your own job description. Most entrepreneurs never get around to that simple and obvious task. Their job description is dictated by whatever is necessary for the business to function on any given day. They take on responsibilities for which they are less than ideally suited, and then expect to perform them all well.

Your first task is to define your role in your business. Until you have done that, it is impossible to define the duties of the farmers who work around you. As long as you continue to waste your creative energy on things at which you are ineffective or unskilled, you can't focus on your most important job—hunting!

Start by writing a description of your job duties today. This isn't a time management exercise, but it *is* efficiency training. Once you have written them down, keep it on your desk or near you for a week or two. When you find yourself doing something that isn't on the list, add it.

You now have a fairly complete list of everything you do in your company. Go over it with a highlighter and mark the things you *like* to do. **Hunters can't afford to waste energy on farming tasks**

I am deliberately not telling you to mark the things you are good at. Why? Because most entrepreneurs will say, "Well, I'm good at that, even though I don't like it." At the risk of deflating your ego, no one is really, really good at something he doesn't like doing. Just because you are currently the best in your company at something does not mean that you should be the one doing it.

If you are like most business owners, you will mark about 20% of your tasks and duties as things you enjoy doing. If you are a typical hunter, these will be the creative aspects of your job, like developing new products, ideas, customers, or systems. It's likely that those are the parts of the business that made you want to own a company in the first place. The other 80% of your time is spent on doing the things you have to do. What would be the impact on your business if you spend 80% of your time working on the things that you like?

Most of us won't get to that 80% mark. Even 40% would be a doubling of time spent on entrepreneurial activities. Those are the things that only you can do, because they are what define your business and its culture. What would be the impact of doubling your time on what you do best? What if you could triple it? Do you think you would be happier? Would you make more money?

Calvin Coolidge said, "We can't do everything at once, but we can do something at once." This is something you can do immediately to start down the road of working less and enjoying it more.

Imagine the effect of working for the next year spending double the current time doing the jobs you enjoy the most. Compare that to the results that you currently generate because of those activities only you can do. (Not the ones you *have* to do!) What would happen to your business? Would sales grow? Would profits grow? By how much?

Compound that growth rate over the next five years. Visualize a business where you are not bogged down in new management duties as you grow. You will continue to have twice the time to do what you enjoy the most. Where would your business be five years from now?

Here is an illustration of the exercise. You own a company that delivers $1,000,000 a year in service work. You currently develop the relationships with new customers, and then hand them off to your service department or technicians to maintain. With you in that role, your business is growing at 10% a year. Let's presume that doubling your time in that area would allow you to grow your business by 20% per year.

After five years of 10% growth, you would own a company that sold just over $1,600,000 annually. At a 20% growth rate, its revenue would be almost $2,500,000! Is it worth it to jettison some farmer chores for an additional 60% growth?

What would your company look like? How big would your offices need to be? How many people would you employ? How many customers would you serve? That is the company you should be planning to lead. It will be a company that you enjoy, and one that you'd anticipate going to every day with pleasure and excitement.

Now, draw an organizational chart that includes all the managers who would report to you in this company. The titles for these positions aren't important, but the job descriptions are. Those job descriptions are made up of the 80% of your tasks and duties that you need to get rid of.

Prioritize the things you most want to delegate. I would start with the things I like the least, but you may prefer to begin with the things that take you the most time. Of course, you won't have all those boxes filled at once, but you can determine which position is next in line for staffing. It is likely that you'll combine two sets of duties in one position at first, and then separate them out when each becomes a job in its own right.

Now, sit back and visualize yourself spending 80% of your time on the things you like to do best. How does your day begin? When does it end? Do you really need to come into the office every day? How does that feel?

If you focus on being a hunter, that day will come. Right now, however, it is time to stop daydreaming and get back to work.

Celebrate Being a Hunter

Being a hunter is something to be proud of. We aren't superior to the vast majority of farmers out there. After all, without farming we would not have modern society. Hunters are just *different*. We have always been a small minority of the population. Just because most folks have forgotten their traditional dependence on hunters doesn't mean that it has ended.

Think about it. There are roughly 180 million working adults in the United States. There are approximately 9 million small business owners with between 2 and 500 employees. Even if small business provides only 40% of total employment, it means 72 million workers are dependent on the hunters for their job. If you include families, that extrapolates to at least 125 million people who need small business owners for their survival, or an average of 14 people for every entrepreneur.

Every business owner is acutely aware of the employees, spouses, children, and other dependents that rely on his or her decisions for their welfare. That sense of responsibility weighs heavily.

> Hunters can farm, but farmers can't hunt

Some people seem to believe that entrepreneurs are lucky to have employees and that they should be required by law to do more for them at every opportunity. They have forgotten one of the oldest truths in human society: Hunters can farm, but farmers can't hunt.

PART II: The Hunter Organization

Chapter 6

Rise of the Farmers

HUNTERS AREN'T FARMERS. For the past 3,000 years, however, society has placed increasing pressure on them to become just that. Big business is a mirror of the society in which it operates. Big business is farming. Small business is hunting. The problem with most advice for small business owners is that it tells them to run their companies like big businesses. Small companies mirror the personality of their owners.

The Farming Cycle

Farming is a cyclical vocation. Farmers plow and plant in the spring, tend the crops through the summer, and harvest in the fall. They spend winters repairing equipment and making other preparations for the next spring. The crop lifecycle is so dominant in farming communities that most agrarian societies paid no attention to calendars until the 18th century. Calendars were only needed by academics and government. The first day of spring on a calendar means nothing to a farmer if the ground is still too frozen to plow. He doesn't wait for the calendar to tell him to get started on the planting season — if the ground has thawed, it is time.

Similarly, big organizations run on a budget cycle. Anyone who deals with large corporations or government entities can tell you about the budget cycle. Assemble data from past years (look at how previous harvests fared), develop projections for the coming year (check the Farmer's Almanac for anticipated weather), issue a budget (plant), generate revenues and control expenses to meet the budget (water and weed), and tally the results (harvest). Then start the process again.

Agriculture supported more complex tribal structures by providing a more dependable food supply than that from hunting alone. Farming became the central activity in the tribe. ("You can't go hunting today, it's time to plant!") Large organizations function in much the same way. When the budget is due, it isn't time to go off on an R&D project, or start brainstorming about new market opportunities. Those activities have their place. Everything has its place.

> Hunters don't think in cycles; they are linear

According to US Small Business Administration statistics, small businesses account for 99.7% of all companies, 50% of the gross domestic product, and 44% of *non-farm* private payroll. If three-tenths of a percent of all businesses employ 56% of the private sector workers, and another 14% of all employees work for the government, is it surprising that a farming mentality dominates most of what we do?

The agricultural cycle that produced a dependable food supply became the schedule that governed all other activities. There is no inherent reason to use a twelve-month calendar to define a business year. Many businesses in the hospitality industry keep their books using a thirteen "month" calendar of equal four-week periods. Some of my clients run distribution companies using thirteen-week "quarters" to track key metrics between comparable periods. They pay little attention to the calendar month in which a quarter begins or ends.

Hunters do not function in repetitive cycles. They focus on a goal and move forward to achieve it. As soon as an objective is completed, they seek the next objective. They don't stop to congratulate themselves on being "ahead of schedule" in life.

Some entrepreneurs focus *only* on the next goal, neglecting even the most basic repetitive tasks. In fact, many of the entrepreneurs that I work with are sloppy about their bookkeeping. They produce profit and loss statements weeks, and sometimes months, after the end of a period. Balance sheets are only reviewed annually. Yet their businesses thrive, and are financially successful.

Their companies don't have budgets, and many don't have a written business plan. How are they successful when they ignore the basic tenets of good financial management?

In most cases, these owners are well aware of their current financial situation. They know how much they have in the bank, what orders are coming in, how much inventory is on hand, and who owes them money. They focus on running the business *today*. They believe, not incorrectly, that controlling the key components of the business on a day-to-day basis will inevitably generate good long-term results.

Financial reports are historical measurement tools, focused on what happened in the past. Entrepreneurs tend to discount them because they already know what happened last month. Their bank account or accounts receivable reflect that quite clearly. Why put a lot of effort into documenting what you already know?

Financial reports are the modern equivalent of game that's been brought back to the tribe. Modern hunters focus on the next deal, the next kill, because they know what the business needs to thrive *tomorrow*.

In our peer boards, we always begin each year by setting some overall goals. The first two are revenue and profitability targets. At the end of the year, we review those goals to see how each member fared in comparison to their objectives of a year before. Many members are surprised at having surpassed their objectives without realizing it. "Really?" they say. "Is that *all* I thought I would do this year?"

For an entrepreneur, goals are things to be pursued, attained, and then moved past. He has an eye on the next level long before reaching the current one. If it comes quickly, then the focus is on how to maximize the favorable conditions to do more. If it comes slowly, then the focus is on how to improve performance to reach it in spite of setbacks. He feels no joy in making 85% of the objective.

Business owners seldom stop to celebrate. I've never heard one say, "We reached our annual target two months early. I'm telling everyone to take it easy until the end of the year."

Measuring your business according to an agricultural calendar farming cycle has limited value. With today's inexpensive computers and software, there is no reason why you can't build a measuring system that is custom designed for the cycle of your business. Measuring your company by its own unique rhythm can help you to maintain your focus where it needs to be, on growing your business.

Small Business and Big Government

Big government understands big business, much as wheat farmers understand melon farmers. The two farmers may have different needs and desired outcomes, but their processes are essentially identical. Similarly, large organizations with thousands of employees understand each other, whether they are in the public or the private sector.

Returning to the US Small Business Administration statistics, since 1990, businesses with fewer than 500 employees created 67% of all the new jobs in America. Following the Great Recession of 2009 and the stubbornly high unemployment that followed, both political parties became newly aware of the entrepreneur's role in creating jobs, and called for government programs to help small business succeed.

Washington politicians' most popular method of showing support for small business is to increase the SBA's lending guaranty authority. They get credit for theoretically injecting billions of dollars into the small business economy.

Debt is not capital. A small business owner typically does not borrow to expand when his company isn't generating cash flow. He doesn't hire when revenues are down. The idea that small business lending is somehow a direct job creation machine is a myth perpetuated for political convenience.

The capital available for expansion in a small company comes from ownership investment, and ownership investment comes from profits. Some business owners have taken enough from their companies to be able to reinvest when times are tough, but most are reinvesting as they go. The public markets appear opaque and indecipherable compared to their own businesses. "I'd rather put my money where I can control it," is a common claim of entrepreneurs. When times are tough, they have neither personal capital nor profits to pump back into their enterprises.

A giant organization can use debt to maintain liquidity when profits are down. If the strategic plan calls for opening a new facility, expanding markets, or hiring more employees, large corporations can borrow the money to do it. Big companies have an asset base and (relatively) predictable profits to leverage. When the government increases lending capacity to entrepreneurs, they are trying to apply big business logic to small companies.

At the deepest point of the Great Recession, one local banker told me proudly that they were still lending to small business. I asked what kind of SBA loans they were making for expansion. Here is how he put it:

> "Let's say you own a profitable dry cleaning operation and you are using absolutely every bit of capacity you have. You own $300,000 worth of equipment free and clear and you want to purchase $200,000 more to meet customer demand. If you pledge the $300,000 in assets and have $100,000 in cash as a down payment, we will lend you the remaining $100,000 for the purchase."

That was an actual conversation. He wasn't kidding. He was proudly telling me that the bank would share risk with an entrepreneur for 20% of his investment. They felt secure with a four to one cushion. The business owner could put up everything he owned to cover the loan with five dollars of value for every dollar borrowed. In turn, the bank could apply for an SBA guarantee to cover 60% of that borrowed dollar. The bank's exposure would be reduced to 8% of the total value of the assets. (Plus they would demand the owner's personal guarantee!) That was their comfort level for financing a small business.

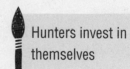

Hunters invest in themselves

With "help" like that, it is not surprising that so many small business owners feel that bankers (and the government regulating the bankers) don't understand them. It isn't deliberate. They are merely large organizations applying their farmer logic to hunters.

Educating Farmers

Farmers run our educational system. That is not a criticism; it's merely a fact. Teachers have to engage in the same cycle year after year. They prepare for a new "crop" (they actually use this term) of students each year. They manage them through a prescribed cycle of learning, measure the results, and send them on their way to make room for the next year group.

In fact, the school calendar is another cyclical timetable that was originally dictated by the agricultural calendar. Classes start after harvest time, there is a break in the spring for planting, and teaching is suspended in summer when labor was traditionally needed most on the farm. Schools in the southern United States tend to begin and end classes earlier than those in the north, because the warmer climate there dictates an earlier growing season.

Just as school schedules are determined by an outdated farming calendar, student achievement is measured by how well each crop performs on standardized tests. There is some inherent logic to standardizing, (you can't have kids deciding that $2 + 2 = 5$), but the drive for measurable results has become a powerful impetus for conformity at all costs. As a result, young hunters in the classroom are often marked as outliers; people who don't fit in.

When my son started second grade, the teacher called us in a few days after school began. "I think John needs some medication," she said. "He is disruptive in class." When asked to describe his behaviors, she went on. "He seems to understand when a lull in the lesson presents the perfect opportunity to make a wry comment. He is very funny, and makes the whole class laugh."

I was stunned and enraged. My son was being clever and bright. Only in the second grade, he already understood humor, timing, and context; and she wanted me to put him on drugs to *stop* it? That is when I realized that the driving purpose of our school system has become as much about conformity as it has about learning.

Anyone with a rambunctious child has probably heard the same. He was running in the playground. She pushed somebody. He talks too loudly. She doesn't pay attention.

My problem behavior at that age was a bit different. I attended an elementary school that shared its parking lot with the public library. I would sneak away from recess to the library. Unfortunately, I would become engrossed in a book, and often didn't hear the bell that signaled the start of class. After multiple sessions with my mother, the teacher finally settled on a practical approach. She simply asked the librarian to find me when the bell rang and send me back.

I was fortunate to have a "problem behavior" that was difficult for a teacher to criticize. (It was also long before a child missing for fifteen minutes triggered an automatic police report.) If instead my fascination had been going to the stream to catch frogs, or building structures in the nearby woods, I wonder how understanding they would have been. I think the system was much harder on the budding scientists and engineers than it was on me.

Our educational system has become a training ground for farmers for a variety of complex reasons. There is the looming threat of litigation in a society that has come to believe that every mishap is someone's fault; blame must be placed and penalties assessed.

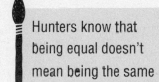

Hunters know that being equal doesn't mean being the same

That creates pressure to have quiet classrooms, no running in the schoolyard, no pushing, and *absolutely* no dodge ball! Farmers in government and business demand measurements of overall educational success to determine career advancement and budget allocations, so schools focus on attaining mass improvements in mediocrity.

What if schools tracked the contributions of their graduates to the gross national product? Shouldn't the impact of a Steve Jobs or a Jeff Bezos count far more than a few tenths of a point toward grade-level math? Perhaps, but it flies in the face of, "All men are created equal," one of the most hallowed phrases in America. Hunters who grow frustrated with waiting for others to catch up know the truth. We may all be created equal, but we aren't all created the *same*.

We have developed a system that encourages the development of farmers from early childhood onward. History focuses on the dates instead of the leadership lessons. Literature focuses on the classics, rather than the radical books that changed the world. Even the programs that teach children the basics of business focus on the math, not on the inspiration. Kids who can't or won't conform are a problem. If they are too much of a problem, they can be medicated.

It is no wonder that so many successful entrepreneurs lower their voices and look away when they tell me, "I'm a little bit ADD."

Chapter 7
Managing Without Farming

HUNTERS, LIKE FARMERS, need some measurements to help them understand the big picture. A good farmer will go into the fields each day to check the health of his crop. He checks the size of the leaves, the depth of the roots, the height of the corn, the moisture in the soil, or whether the wheat sprouted. These are historical results, measuring past activity.

The hunter looks at more predictive measures. Is the weather turning colder? That may mean game is migrating. Has it rained recently, thus making tracking easier? Those are variables that help the hunter determine how likely he is to be successful. Hunters seek measurements that tell them what to expect, not what happened yesterday.

Entrepreneurs have limited patience for detailed reports, but instinct and on-the-job observation alone aren't enough to really understand what is going on in a company. They need information that is easily collected, easily understood, and predictive.

There are three simple methodologies that are underutilized in running an entrepreneurial business. These three tools help many report-resistant hunters monitor their companies without getting mired down in historical reporting or excessive detail. They are *flash reports, common sizing, and graphs.*

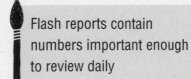

Flash reports contain numbers important enough to review daily

Flash Reports

Flash reports, as you might guess from their name, are statistics that tell you in a flash what is going on in your business. Unless your business involves only a few transactions each month, they are worth producing daily.

Vanessa Wheeler owned Priority Information Services, a litigation support company providing computerized document organization and exhibits for trial lawyers. Vanessa was a Technician, starting the company after an early career as a Sheriff's Deputy and then as a salesperson for a company providing litigation support. Vanessa had no business background, and her first love was working in the courtroom.

Like many entrepreneurs, Vanessa built the company through hard work and personal talent. She had a feel for the flow of a trial and the attorney's mindset, anticipating upcoming questions and necessary exhibits. Launching the right document or the right diagram on screens the moment an attorney asks for it can make a big impact on a jury. An attorney can easily lose the flow of his argument while a technician fumbles through files looking for the right exhibit (not surprising, since virtually all courtroom attorneys are hunters).

Although Vanessa was a wizard technician, her weeks spent working with attorneys in big trials were all-consuming. Each day would wind up with a conference between Vanessa and the attorneys, discussing what had happened in the courtroom that day, and planning tactics for the next session. Vanessa would then return to her hotel to prepare support materials for the next day's hearing. That work often took until the early morning hours, leaving time for only a quick nap before starting again.

Unfortunately, she would return to her company after a lengthy absence to find that her fifteen employees had missed a deadline, or had brought in little additional work to supplement her high-dollar services. Vanessa was stuck in a Technician's doom loop. Her own talents provided the highest margin work, but they pulled her away from managing the rest of the business.

Since Vanessa had no formal business education, her monthly financial statements seemed akin to a foreign language. Besides, they only told her what she already knew. Valerie, Vanessa's office manager (and her sister) developed a solution. Every morning, as her very first duty, Valerie delivered a set of figures from the previous day's activities. They were:

- cash balance in the bank
- outstanding checks
- production billed
- new orders
- collections
- total outstanding accounts receivable

Was this flash report the entire story of what was happening in Vanessa's company? Of course not, but look at what she had. Using her extensive knowledge of her own business, Vanessa could quickly extrapolate the company's liquidity, sales activity, employee productivity, receivables ageing and future production capacity.

"Manage what you measure," requires forward-looking metrics

In a business that depended both on low margin production work (document retrieval, scanning, indexing) as well as high-priced, but intermittent, skilled work (trial support) the daily flash report was effective. It gave Vanessa more pertinent and more actionable information than any monthly statement.

Vanessa never did get comfortable with traditional financial reporting, but her flash reports provided enough information to run her business successfully for twenty years, until she sold it to a larger, multi-market competitor.

The factors in your flash report should be easily generated and consistently measured. You can choose to track a variety of metrics, but I recommend no more than five for a daily report. Too many numbers start to blend together, and you may tend to skip over those that are less variable until they stand out as a problem.

The most important metrics to track are those that help you anticipate upcoming challenges. Contract backlog, weeks of production scheduled, leads generated, and appointments made are all indicators that can help you understand what is *going* to happen. "Managing what you measure" for a hunter should mean forward looking metrics. Build your flash report to focus on things you will need to manage, not to track how you managed things in the past.

Common Sizing

Common size reports are simple, and just what their name suggests. You compile your operating numbers and arrange them in a format with a common measurement, usually as a ratio to total sales. Divide each component of revenue and expenses by total revenue, giving a percentage figure for every line item.

Common size profit and loss statements are available in every business bookkeeping program from the most basic versions of QuickBooks to industry specific applications. You can also ask your CPA to prepare them for you.

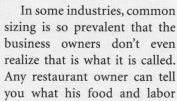

Common size reports allow easy tracking of expense changes over time

In some industries, common sizing is so prevalent that the business owners don't even realize that is what it is called. Any restaurant owner can tell you what his food and labor costs are in percentages. They know what their targets are, and track them constantly.

In many restaurants, the labor costs are such a large component of profitability that managers review them *hourly*. Any slowing in the number of diners is cause for an immediate reduction in staff to maintain the targeted expense ratio.

In distribution and manufacturing, where the cost of product is high in proportion to the selling price, the gross margin percentage is a vital indicator. A successful manufacturer or distributor knows what gross margin percentage is required to cover expenses and leave an appropriate profit.

Surprisingly, many businesses only use common sizing with one or two key indicators. In doing so, they are neglecting one of the best tools for making their financial statements useful and for keeping an eye on the bottom line.

Here is an example: Last year, your company enjoyed $2,197,645 in sales. This year it was $2,742,098. Your printing and copying costs last year were $86,766. This year you spent 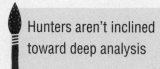 $104,200. Were your costs better or worse? If you are a typical hunter, I probably lost your attention about halfway through this example.

Hunters aren't inclined toward deep analysis

Despite a more than $17,000 increase in printing costs, the actual percentage of revenue spent on printing dropped from 3.95% to 3.8%. Presumably, that left .15% of $2.7 million, or just over $4,000 more, for your bottom line. Isn't it easier and more actionable to know that printing costs dropped from 3.95% to 3.8%, than that they went from $86,766 to $104,200? Which method of reporting gives you better information about your business? In an instant, you can understand whether data is good, bad, or not worth worrying about.

It is not enough just to know whether you made money or not, you have to understand why. Common sizing lets you look at two periods (weeks or months or years or whatever works best for your business) side-by-side, and see where profit was made or lost. Armed with better information, you can focus your energy on the things that matter most.

When one of our clients complains about eroding profits, the first thing we do is place the last few years' common sized profit and loss statements side-by-side in a spreadsheet. It takes only a few minutes to look at expense trends across several years, and it can be hugely enlightening.

Let's say the client's operating profit has dropped from 10% to 5% over the last three years. Looking at common sizing, we discover that his shipping expense as a percent of sales has increased by a bit less than 1% per year. We have quickly identified *half* of the lost profit problem!

The answer may be simple, such as increasing minimum order size or adding a handling charge. It may be intractable because of competitive pressures. Analyzing by common size doesn't fix the problems; it just zeros in on them so you can make better decisions.

Hunters aren't inclined toward deep analysis. No one ever economized his way to greater revenues. Cost control decisions are important, but delving into historical numbers shouldn't come at the expense of business development. Common sizing will tell you *what* to analyze. It is quick and clear, indicating in moments whether an area needs your attention. Use it often and you will have more time to do the things you do best.

Graphs

Everyone processes information in one of three ways, visually, auditorily, or kinesthetically, that is, by sight, sound, or feeling. Of the population as a whole, 85% use vision as their primary information-processing tool. For hunters, I think the number is closer to 100% (good eyesight being an obvious natural selector for successful hunters). Why then, do we insist on running our businesses using the most non-visual information possible?

> No one ever economized his way to greater revenues

Numbers are abstract. You have to look at them, and then process some internal frame of reference to make sense of them. Few people have the visual memory capability to assess numbers. How much is $1,000,000? What does it look like as a pile of $1 bills? How about as a pile of $20 bills? Are you really visualizing a stack that is 95% smaller than the first one? How big is that?

Graphs are readily available in every spreadsheet program, in many bookkeeping programs, and even in popular word processing programs. You can easily set them up to track days, weeks, pay periods, months, quarters or any other data set that makes sense for your business.

I use line graphs. It is tempting to dive into the many options that today's software allows. There are bar graphs and pie graphs and exploded pies and 3D and radar graphs. I've even seen versions where you get a "dashboard" tool made up of circular speedometer gauges that show how close to a redline you are. None are better than **Numbers are abstract; hunters need visual information** an old-fashioned line graph for showing you the most important thing, whether your numbers are trending up or down.

Remember the KISS (Keep It Simple, Stupid!) principle. Don't try to graph *everything* that happens in your business. Start with the numbers that mean the most to you; sales, backlog, leads, labor, margin, accounts receivable days, or anything that will help you to understand what is happening at a glance. It probably makes the most sense to graph common size percentages or the numbers from your flash report.

Most importantly, *you* shouldn't be the one generating the graphs. The objective of graphing, as with the two other methodologies discussed previously, is to make it easier for you to have a handle on your business, not to assign yourself a farming task. The simple arithmetic exercise of coming up with the numbers and putting them into the computer belongs to a farmer. You need your time to hunt.

Chapter 8
Leading Hunters

FARMING HAS ONE INHERENT ADVANTAGE over hunting—economies of scale. To plant and grow a successful crop, you only need one person who really knows what he is doing. One individual can decide when to plant, when to irrigate, and when to harvest. The rest of the farmers merely execute the tasks.

You can put an experienced tiller, for example, in the first row of a field. Then you can line up the rest of the tribe, young and old, male and female, in the rest of the rows and say, "Watch him. Do what he is doing," and the resulting work will be more or less acceptable.

Hunting doesn't work like that. You can't take along the weak or the stupid or anyone who can only do half the job. Each hunter in the group has to be roughly at the level of the rest.

A hunter faces a conundrum. If he is successful, the tribe (or business) grows; but the hunter can only bring in a limited amount by himself. So the more successful he is, the more he needs additional hunters to sustain the tribe.

Salespeople

In business, that usually means salespeople. Few of us have a business model so exceptional that we don't need to recruit customers. If you are lucky enough to have such a business, you can skip the remainder of this chapter. The rest of us have to go out and find the customers who will buy from us.

Unless your company is going to be permanently limited to the revenue you can generate by yourself, you have to hire salespeople in order to grow.

Salespeople are a lot like ancient hunters. Envision a prehistoric tribe living in a big cave. The hunters come in and throw down a large dead animal. Then they sit around the fire while the meal is prepared and tell everyone the details of how they made the kill. They bask in their success, while the skinners and cooks grumble that the hunters never do anything useful.

Successful salespeople are employed hunters

Flash forward 7,000 years and picture salespeople standing around the coffee machine after closing a big deal. Things really haven't changed that much.

By nature, hunters think independently. They need to be led, not merely managed. Too many business owners try to *manage* their sales forces. It's easy to mire a sales force in reporting and tracking activities, when what you really want them to do is go out and *sell*. Why is it axiomatic that you should not make your best salesperson into a sales manager? It's because most of the time you are ruining a great hunter by forcing him to be a reluctant farmer.

It is hard for a business owner to hand off the revenue-generating functions of the business. They fear the expense of an uncontrolled or ineffective representative calling on their customers. An underperforming salesperson is costly in several ways. Not only is the expense of maintaining him not justified, there is the lost opportunity of potential customers who might have bought if he was more capable. To reduce that risk, owners create systems to manage the salespeople. They have processes to manage all the other functions of their companies, so it seems logical to use them to manage the sales function.

That is a farmer's solution. Huge organizations with hundreds or thousands of salespeople can afford to have a bell curve of success among their sales personnel. Some will be poor performers, most will perform well enough to pay their way, and a few will actually generate most of the profits. A small business owner can't afford to carry *any* low performers. Each salesperson must be individually profitable.

Many entrepreneurs, especially those who built companies around their personal selling skills, try to be like the tiller in the first row of the cornfield. "Watch me," they say, "and do what I do." Their salespeople mimic their behavior. They make a specified number of calls, they fill in information on the company's customer relationship management (CRM) system, they send out marketing materials, and—they fail.

Great salespeople don't need much in the way of management. Andy Goldman owns a "pipe and drape" company that provides infrastructure for trade shows and conferences. They have relationships with professional societies and associations to deliver the aisle dividers, carpet, tables, chairs, wastebaskets and the other paraphernalia needed for a typical business exhibition. Relationships are long-term; if you do a good job for the client, you will handle their events year after year.

Industry shows frequently move around from city to city each year. The convention business is a bit like a traveling circus. The event might be in **Promotion to sales manager frequently ruins a great hunter** Chicago this year, San Diego next year, and Orlando the year after that. To keep a good customer, you have to not only go wherever they go, but also to bring along everything they might need.

As anyone who has exhibited at a trade show knows, there is frequently something you forgot, or didn't realize you needed until you set up your booth. You suddenly want an extra table, a wastebasket, some chairs or a power outlet. You go back to the trade show manager's office and order it (at an exorbitant price). Not surprisingly, those last minute orders can generate as much as 50% of the management company's profits from every show.

When Andy's employees pack the trucks for an event, they are always guessing about what exhibitors might order on the show floor. They check last year's records, total up preorders, review the paid attendance for this year, and frankly, then they stick a finger in the air to test the prevailing winds. Have trade shows in general had a lot of last minute exhibitors or cancellations this year? Are people scrimping on the little luxuries or are they outfitting their booths with everything they can hold?

Then Andy's employees load up a fleet of tractor-trailers with a few miles of carpet, pipe, and drape, throw in a few hundred or a few thousand extra tables, chairs, poster stands and whatever else might be needed, and send off the crew on a cross-country jaunt to the event.

Like an airline or a hotel, you can only sell what you have, and if you brought too much inventory, any price you can get is better than not using it at all. If you run out of tables, you have both angry customers and missing profits. If you brought too many tables, you are better off renting them for half price than leaving them in the truck.

Andy employs two kinds of salespeople. Those who call on trade associations for event contracts are called salespeople, and the ones responsible for half the profits are called show managers. Show managers are the ones who rent the stuff that gets ordered on the floor. There is little inventory control. If a customer pays with cash, who is to say whether a table was out on the show floor or sitting in the back of the truck for three days?

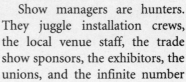

A small business can't afford any low performers

Show managers are hunters. They juggle installation crews, the local venue staff, the trade show sponsors, the exhibitors, the unions, and the infinite number of things that can go wrong when there are thousands of people spending huge sums of money to do business in a compressed time frame.

Andy's system for handling the show managers is straightforward. They get a percentage of everything that is sold or rented on-site. It is a major part of their compensation. If they are caught even once pocketing an undeclared dime of the proceeds, they are immediately terminated.

It is a simple system for hunters. Do it right and make a lot of money, or skim some and risk never making that money again. It was effective

 Let hunters do their jobs without detailed paperwork

enough that for years Andy's company didn't bother with management systems or tracking show floor rentals. The show managers had enough to do without adding detailed paperwork to their workload. They were left free to do their jobs, and were very successful at it.

The event salespeople have the more traditional job of calling on the sponsoring organizations to sell contracts for running the shows. Trade show locations and support contracts are typically negotiated two or three years in advance. It is a long sales cycle from introduction, to contract, to event; and a salesperson that had to live on commission alone would starve long before he saw a paycheck.

For that reason, Andy always paid his salespeople a straight salary. They brought in enough work to keep the company growing steadily and everyone was happy. Andy's TAB peer group, however, kept encouraging him to add an incentive to the base he was paying.

Finally, and with great trepidation, Andy developed a plan that paid recurring commissions for repeat customers, along with a hefty bonus on new business. He first presented it to his top salesman, asking him to look it over and give feedback on what he thought of it. Andy was quite ready to throw the whole plan out if his premier hunter objected.

The next day Andy asked the salesman if he had a chance to look through the plan, and whether he had any comments. "Just one, boss," said the salesman. "Thanks for the raise!"

Every action has a reaction. A few months later, it was Andy's turn to update his fellow peer group members. "I'm sorry I ever listened to you guys," he sighed, (plainly employing his very dry sense of humor). "I had a nice company. Steady business, good profits. Now these salespeople have gone crazy! I'm constantly buying additional equipment, and I'm going to be forced to build a bigger warehouse!"

Sometimes the life of an entrepreneur can be cruel.

Never Terminate a Salesperson

Andy Goldman's story is a humorous look at the effect of giving salespeople the right incentives. The truth is, you can lead a salesman to customers, but you can't make him sell. He is motivated (and skilled) or he isn't.

How do you motivate a salesman? Most need enough money to live on before they start generating new sales, while business owners usually want to pay for performance. The number of pay and incentive schemes I've seen would fill another book, but there is a simple approach to balancing guarantees and incentives.

I originally got this concept from my friend and client Kirk Francis, the owner of Cross Financial Services. Kirk has owned his company for over twenty years, but earlier in his career, he was the youngest branch manager in history for a national stock brokerage. He has hired and trained hundreds of salespeople, and he has a simple formula.

In the Francis Curve, the horizontal axis represents time and the vertical axis is sales compensation. The solid line is guaranteed pay, and the dotted line is commission.

First, determine how much time it should take a salesperson to be effective in your business. It could be days, months, or perhaps even years, depending on your normal sales cycle. You guarantee a living wage for that time.

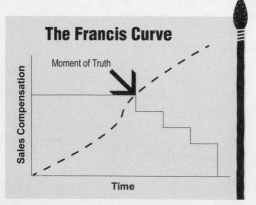

The base can be a salary, a draw, or the recurring commissions generated from existing assigned accounts. The key is that it has a limited time frame, which is agreed upon between you and the employee at the outset. When that date is reached, the guarantee ceases.

The dotted line is based on expected commissions as the salesperson becomes more successful. They aren't paid in addition to the base, because you are still investing in the employee. Where the two lines cross in the future is when the salesperson gives up the guarantee, and begins his "eat what you kill" career.

With base and time frames structured appropriately at the outset, there are few reasons why a real hunter should fall short. As the expiration date for the guarantee approaches, many will argue for an extension. If you agree to change the compensation agreement, you are starting all over. There are always obstacles to any salesperson's targets; they are called customers. His job, by definition, is overcoming those obstacles.

If you refuse to extend the date (and you should), a salesperson who is close, and has confidence that he will soon hit the target, will assume the risk of a temporarily reduced income for the rewards that are just around the corner. Those who seek an indefinite extension until they make it aren't really hunters.

If you stick to the plan, you will never have to fire an unproductive salesperson. They will fire themselves. In fact, the really good ones often ask to go on straight commission *before* the deadline, because they can make more income from incentives than they do from salary.

Hunters Who Don't Hunt

There is another type of hunter who is needed in every strong organization. He is a Second in Command (SIC).

You may have more than one SIC, but each of them reports directly to you. They are not hunters in the sense that they go out after game, like salespeople, but they still work with an "eat what you kill" attitude.

A good Second in Command thinks like you. He is driven to build and grow the company without your constant oversight. You can produce goals and objectives for an SIC, but they should only frame the results you seek, not how to achieve them. A Second in Command who is really a hunter shares in the financial results of the company. He is motivated by the bottom line.

Second in Commands come in two versions. One is the person who is expected to handle the major management tasks of running the business that you don't take on yourself. That SIC should have skills and expertise that compliment yours. The other type, which I call an SIT, or Successor in Training, is expected to eventually assume *all* of your responsibilities in the business.

You could easily have both types in your company. If you are personally oriented toward business development, for example, you might have a controller who is your SIC, and a sales manager who is an SIT. Developing either (and preferably both) into valued and fully competent components of your team may require that you resist your hunter tendencies for some time. You have to let them implement their own solutions to problems, and occasionally watch them fail.

The most frequent complaint I hear from business owners about their employees is, "They don't think like me." They become frustrated by managers whom they've raised to a level of responsibility, but who can't make sound decisions, solve problems, or work through the long-term implications of their actions.

As we discussed in Chapter 3, most entrepreneurs owe their success to creative tenacity. They solve problems, and keep solving them until they get the result they seek. They are the masters of chaos, figuring out how to get around problems when others freeze in the headlights. It is a necessary trait, and one that is hard to find in an employee.

Many business owners believe that their problem-solving ability is their biggest contribution to the business. They complain about making all of the decisions, but the fact is, they like it. They get the little rush that comes with taking care of something only they could handle. They enjoy giving out answers and the security of being the one who *knows*.

If you are going to develop a hunter to help you run your business, you have to learn how not to solve problems. People need to figure things out for themselves in order to really learn. It may cost you money, and it certainly will cost you some time. Allowing room for employee self-education doesn't mean that you step away from decisions completely. After all, you have to be vigilant that an employee isn't embarking on an organization-threatening course of action. Unless you hold back, however, and surrender the satisfaction of fixing things instantly, you will never have another decision maker that you can depend on.

Owners complain that employees "don't think like me"

Another problem entrepreneurs have in developing effective SICs and SITs is their tendency to abdicate rather than delegate. Delegation is the assignment of responsibilities with a *built-in* feedback loop. You have a check and balance system for tracking results. There are clear parameters to work within, and no major action is taken without final approval.

Abdication is surrendering control completely. Decisions are made without your input, or without even knowing what was decided until the results come in. Many business owners are so relieved to have a competent manager that they let go of the reins far too early in the development process. Just because someone says, "I've got it handled," doesn't always mean he does.

One owner of a service firm I work with had taken on a major role with a charity about which he felt passionate. His business was doing well and he entered into a search for a Second in Command who could run operations while the owner devoted most of his time to community service.

The chosen SIC appeared to be an ideal candidate, with ample experience in roles that carried considerable responsibility. The staff members were thrilled to have someone to direct them every day, and gave the new executive high marks. When the owner asked how things were going, he was told "Great!" The business hired new salespeople, and began negotiations to acquire another location in an adjacent town. The owner threw himself into his community service, secure in the knowledge that his business was managed better than he would have done himself.

Toward the end of his first year on the job, the SIC asked to schedule a meeting with the owner, me, and the company's CPA to go over his plans for the coming year. In that meeting, he presented reams of reports and spreadsheets showing what he had done, along with his projections for the coming year. It took the rest of us some time to fully digest what was represented by all of those charts and spreadsheets, but it came down to a few key items.

First, the company was out of cash, and would not make payroll past the current month without an infusion of at least $100,000 immediately.

Second, the manager had completely drawn down all the credit lines, and had no resources left to tap for working capital.

Finally, implementing the manager's plan for the coming year would require an additional investment of $500,000 and, since he knew this was beyond the owner's financial capability, he recommended that the business be put up for sale as soon as possible to a buyer who could afford to make the investment.

To say that we were all stunned would be a gross understatement. To say that the executive was terminated in very short order would be another.

The owner plunged back into day-to-day management and the business survived. Today, with a new SIC who is more competent (and working with a *much* more attentive owner), it is again growing and profitable.

To say that the owner was at fault for his inattention is, of course, true; but we shouldn't be too quick to criticize. He was an entrepreneur who had built his business for twenty years. Throughout that time, he was the chief salesperson and the sole decision maker. The relief of having a seemingly competent SIC who said "Don't worry, I have everything handled," was so welcome after decades of daily worrying that it was easy to accept at face value.

Ronald Reagan's famous "Trust ... but verify" comment is clearly the rule by which we should run our businesses. There is another line that should be at the top of every entrepreneur's plan to develop a Second in Command: "SPEND MORE TIME." Many attempts to delegate to an SIC fail because we become too dependent on them before they really understand how we *think,* and *why* we make the decisions we do.

When you teach people how to run your business, they have to understand more than what you would do. They have to "grok" *why* you would do it. (Grok is borrowed from Robert Heinlein's science fiction classic "Stranger in a Strange Land." It means to fully absorb into your being so that it becomes a permanent part of who you are. It is the best term I've found for the level of understanding necessary in an SIC.)

Teaching an SIC or an SIT how to run your business is much more than giving them assignments and checking the results. To run your business, he must understand what your perception of quality is, how you want your employees to feel about the company, and what your vision for the future looks like.

If your Second in Command is truly a hunter, he will embrace decision-making. If he is competent and savvy, those decisions will work out pretty well for the most part. However, unless you invest the time to help him grok your business, those decisions will be based on the company he wants to run, not necessarily the one you want to own.

Keeping Hunters

Some business owners stifle their own growth. They want to develop employees who know enough to make the business run, but not quite enough to go into business for themselves.

The majority of entrepreneurs begin as technicians. Lawyers with their own firms start out as lawyers in another firm. Contractors begin as carpenters or electricians. Wholesale distributors were sales reps or resellers. How can you develop true hunters, people who don't need you to survive, but still keep them in your organization?

I have worked with a few companies that function as involuntary business incubators. Every few years an employee leaves to go into competition with his former employer. It happens

Teaching someone to run your business is much more than delegation

repeatedly, but the owner doesn't see the source of the problem. "No one is loyal these days," he says. Or sometimes, "That's the gratitude I get for teaching him everything he knows."

Gratitude is a lousy motivator. It is short-lived and quickly forgotten. If you teach an employee how to do something and he does it well, do you really believe that he looks at the results and says, "I'm just so glad the boss taught me that?" Of course not! He says, "I did a great job on something new that I tried for the first time. I'm pretty darn good!" Let's face it. You would say the same thing.

How do you develop great employees, true hunters — the people who can really help you build your business — without creating a constant stream of new competitors?

> Can your best hunters reach their goals while working for you?

Juan Pablo Cabrera is the CEO of Rooster Industries, a manufacturer of soft goods largely for the construction and home improvement markets. Incentives are concentrated on the "hunters," the top two levels of responsibility among the company's 1,200 employees. They do the most to influence profitability, and have the most at risk regarding their personal compensation.

Level One. These are the leaders. They place the needs of the company high in their life priorities and are responsible for the most crucial decisions in running the business.

Level Two. These are the people who support Level One, and are responsible for executing the business plan. They may not be quite as committed, or handle the same level of decision-making, but they are vital to operations.

If the company achieves its profitability targets, all Level One and Two employees participate in the incentive pool. If the targets are missed, no one receives any bonus.

Level Three and Level Four employees are task-based. They are workers whose incentives are determined by personal productivity

(Level Four), or their supervisors (Level Three) whose compensation is based on the productivity of those whom they supervise.

Juan Pablo says that Level One employees are those who essentially enter into a career contract. Juan Pablo literally refers to them as the employees who "bring the meat." They are the ones he never wants to run the business without. He believes that if you want people to devote all of their productive working years to your business, then you have to offer them a result commensurate with that level of commitment. This requires that you provide a compensation program guaranteeing that by the end of their career, their families will enjoy financial security and a lifestyle that was unimaginable when they first started working for you. The Level One employees are compensated directly on company profitability.

Level Two employees are decision makers. Their choices affect profitability, but they work within a defined scope of authority. Their incentives are customized to reward the right decisions within their areas of responsibility.

If you have a hunter, a *real* hunter, can you reasonably expect him to work indefinitely for an incrementally larger paycheck each year? Do you anticipate that he will be eternally satisfied just to know that he is important to the business, and enjoys your high esteem? If that were true, then most business owner Technicians would still be employed technicians.

Finding, teaching and keeping a hunter is a two-way street. Rooster Industries seeks to keep its critical hunters by reciprocating their commitment to the company with a commitment to their future. If you only make the same promise that you offer to any other employee (show up, do your job, get paid) then you will eventually lose your best hunters. Investing in an SIC or an SIT requires offering something unique. It does not have to be equity ownership, although that is the currency some companies choose. It can be deferred compensation, stock appreciation rights, or vesting in an insurance policy.

Key hunters have ambitions that are similar to yours. Remember, you probably started your business because you wanted to achieve something your employer couldn't provide. You had your own vision of what your life should look like. Top quality employees have visions too. You have to decide whether you can help them accomplish those goals while working for you.

Chapter 9
Managing Farmers

I **N ORDER TO GROW** and be successful, your business probably needs at least a few hunters in addition to you, but no organization is going to work very well if it is comprised entirely of hunters. Trying to build one like that is as big a mistake as building a business of all farmers.

Why? It's *your* company. You take the risks and you make the decisions. An organization with a few hunters who understand your objectives and work in the areas you've assigned to them is stronger. One that has hunters at every level drifts into democracy, if not anarchy. Every hunter-employee should expect some autonomy and decision-making authority. But in the real world, businesses don't run by consensus. They need a single direction and a single vision, and that direction and vision has to be yours.

Fortunately, most employees prefer to be farmers. Remember that less than 3% of the population creates 44% of all the private sector employment and 67% of all new jobs. That ratio of farmers to hunters is twenty or thirty to one. Keeping your farmer employees happy and productive comes from providing them with clear duties that produce reasonably predictable outcomes.

At first glance, this flies in the face of modern management theory that encourages organizations to let their workers be "entrepreneurial." I'm not arguing against empowerment, it is a

A business needs a single vision, and that has to be yours

powerful management tool. You might find, though, that it often isn't as easy as it sounds, and not everyone is capable of accepting it. Some, in fact, are steadfastly against it.

When I owned a medical management company in California, I enrolled in an executive MBA program. Our first trimester focused on organizational behavior, and I enthusiastically embraced the concept of empowering employees.

The medical offices we managed focused on serving senior citizens. I thought health care would be an ideal environment for letting workers at all levels make decisions. I knew that the majority of our employees had chosen the field because they wanted to help people. With such a vocational workforce, I believed that it would be a simple matter to let the staff decide how to "do the right thing" when it came to patients.

We gave each staff member the ability to order equipment without prior approval if they thought it would help a patient. They were retrained to take extra time with patients, and to make special accommodations for infirmities or disabilities. We asked for employee input on redesigning workflows, procedures and room furnishings based on what they saw in their work with patients every day.

One morning I received a call from the office manager at our largest and busiest clinic. Several of the medical assistants there had asked to meet with me, on what they termed a problem of immediate and vital importance. Since we did not want to disrupt the patients' schedules, I arranged to drive over and meet them in the employee break room during their lunch hour.

Medical assistants are the backbone of a primary care practice. Trained in a vocational school or community college, they perform many of the routine but critical tasks in patient care. They take patients back to an exam room, check their vital signs, and register their complaints. They are the chief contact with patients, spending far more time with them than the physicians do. Studies show that patients rank satisfaction based on their interaction with the medical assistants *regardless of the physician's diagnosis or any medical outcome.*

We were fully aware of how important our MAs were. Often, the patients confided in them about issues regarding access to services, or personal problems affecting their treatment plans. The medical assistants were our front line in delivering quality care, and we wanted them to have the flexibility to do their best.

The three medical assistants who met with me were among our most productive performers. They were dependable and knew their

 Farmers don't necessarily embrace flexibility on the job

jobs well. After initial pleasantries, I ask what their concerns were. At first, their responses were vague, describing some discomfort with the "way things were going." I tried to pinpoint their complaint. Was it the supervision, the management, their compensation, or their duties?

Finally, one of them burst out. "We know what you are trying to do with this empowerment stuff," she exclaimed. "We didn't take these jobs to make *decisions*. You are supposed to tell us what to do and we do it. That's the way it has always been and that's all we are going to do, or we will quit."

I asked the other two if they felt the same way and they said that they did. I explained that what we were trying to do might be a little uncomfortable at first, but we were letting them have the authority to deliver better patient care. They replied that it didn't matter, and demanded I promise that any decision-making on their part would cease immediately or they were walking out.

I told them that I understood their issue. Then, still sitting with them at the table, I took out my cell phone and dialed my Director of Operations. "Marcia," I said when she answered. "I need you to find three medical assistants to staff this office for the rest of the day, or we are going to be very shorthanded." (See, it is *good* to have a few hunters on the team!)

I then told the three that I respected them for speaking up. I also respected their decision, and would have the office manager come right in to help them remove any personal belongings from the premises. There was no point in continuing if the way I chose to run our company made them so miserable.

Not everyone embraces flexibility on the job. Some resist it more than others. Sometimes an entrepreneur has difficulty understanding why people prefer to be managed.

My experience is an extreme illustration of resistance to flexibility, but it is not unique. Everybody likes some measure of control over their jobs. The medical assistants were trying to exercise control; although, like many farmers, they hadn't fully thought through all of the possible consequences. More typically, farmers appreciate being included and informed. They like having input in the decision-making process. They enjoy the recognition of asking for their opinion.

However, farmers don't want to be cast into the chaos to figure it all out for themselves. That is a hunter's job. If you read the empowerment books carefully, they advocate sharing responsibility with employees for decision making *within defined parameters*. They don't pretend that you can make farmers into hunters. Empowerment is about letting the farmers help determine their farming methodologies.

Farmers aren't sheep. They're not robots. They are certainly not stupid. They just aren't hunters. They need guidance and support to help them do their jobs well. Helping farmers with systems and measurements they can understand is called management.

Leadership vs. Management

Chapter 8 is titled "Leading Hunters," and Chapter 9 is "Managing Farmers." What is the difference?

A good manager is always a leader. A leader is not always a good manager. Most entrepreneurs prefer building new things to running the day-to-day operations. The owner's preference for the new or novel leads them to think that their employees prefer the same. That is rarely the case.

Leadership is largely a communications skill. It is one thing to have a vision; it is another to be able to enunciate it clearly and succinctly to others. It is still another to express it in a way that makes others excited about buying into it.

Leadership is done from the front. The United States Army has a statistic that they track during wartime. They use it to analyze both their own and foreign troop effectiveness. It is the casualty rate among lieutenants. If the rate is too high, communications and decision making in the field are denigrated. If it is too low, the troops are being committed to battle situations with insufficient leadership. Lieutenants are supposed to be out front, but they are expected to take appropriate caution to preserve their own lives.

A few years ago, my wife and I were vacationing in Vienna, and toured one of the world's great collections of arms and armor in Hofburg Palace. There was an entire room filled with pole weapons. It had spears, pikes, long-axes, lances and halberds. The halberd is a pole with a combination axe and spear point, sometimes including a hook or long blade to balance the axe head.

There was a huge display of halberds, but one in particular drew my attention. Labeled a Sergeant's Halberd, it was dated from the early 1800s. I couldn't figure out why an essentially medieval weapon would still be deployed long after firearms had become the standard issue for troops, and I commented aloud on the puzzle to my wife.

A nearby docent snickered. In response to my inquiring look, he explained, "You must understand, sir. In those days, the sergeants walked *behind* their troops."

You can immediately visualize the situation. Firearms were still relatively new to warfare, and military tactics in the early 1800s had not caught up to the technology. Troops still attacked by walking in formation across open ground.

Anyone who has seen a war movie from that age has only the slightest inkling of the terror such a battle must have generated. The enemy, approaching in formation, fired a volley, simultaneously disappearing in a cloud of smoke. (If movies really duplicated the clouds emitted from black powder muskets, there would be nothing visible left to film.) From out of that cloud, arriving even before the sound of the volley, came balls of lead that randomly cut men down with horrific wounds.

Any sane human being could only think of finding shelter or running away. The sergeants' halberds put a more immediate threat behind the men to force them forward.

Sergeants manage. Lieutenants lead. Lieutenants begin preparation for battle in briefings, where they learn what the objective is, and how their actions will fit into the battle plan. Sergeants point to the objective and tell their men to take it. They are not privy to the grand strategy.

In the early stages of a business, the entrepreneur is a lieutenant. He leads his employees, perhaps lacking even a sergeant to help push them forward. As the business grows, the owner must rise from a battlefield commander to someone who understands the strategy of the entire war. He develops lieutenants under him who understand the plan, and in turn, they develop sergeants to implement it.

If your company has grown larger than about ten employees, it is time to stop dividing your time between leading and management, and to focus exclusively on being a leader. Until you start developing managers under you who can execute the day-to-day work, you are depriving your business of what it most needs to be successful—focused leadership.

Merely making sure that everyone in your business is accomplishing their tasks isn't hunting, but it is where many hunters get bogged down. The business stops growing because your time is limited. Entry-level employees are less productive because you don't have the bandwidth for proper training, and they make errors that cost you additional time and money.

This is the trap I initially find many small business owners in when they become clients. Sales have flattened because they can't figure out how to keep up with their management duties. The answer isn't to manage better. That is a farmer's job. The way to resuscitate growth is to stop managing and start leading.

> **Leaders are in front; managers follow leaders**

The Farmer's Job

Agriculture is cyclical. Till, plant, water, weed, harvest, and repeat. Repetitive work also constitutes between 80% and 90% of all the output of any company.

Some owners, especially those who employ professionals, may disagree. You might think that lawyers, engineers, or programmers deal with unique problems and create unique solutions. While there is some truth to that, those solutions are usually developed according to accepted norms and within defined parameters.

Attorneys draft agreements to comply with existing law. Engineers have to meet building codes, and use proven materials and methods. Programmers write code to accomplish certain objectives and to fit within specific computer languages or legacy programs. Each may have some leeway in their approach and structure, but the boundaries are clear.

An attorney who starts a law firm decides what kind of law he will practice. Whether his interest is in family law, litigation or **Managing farmers is more than just telling them what to do** contracts, the other attorneys who join the firm will practice in that area or one that is complimentary. By striking out on his own, the attorney has changed his viewpoint from cyclical to linear.

Your job as an entrepreneur is to decide what type of work your company will do, not to do all of it. You identify the 85% of work that is repetitive, and teach others how to handle it.

For a Technician, this is the biggest challenge. At some point in their employed career, they were probably one of the best at a specific technical skill. Surrendering that ego-boosting position is hard, but they can't grow a business without doing so.

For the Creators, the difficulty lies in taking the time to teach others how to do things the way they want them done. They naturally want to focus on new initiatives, not the boring old routine of daily operations.

For the Acquirer or the Inheritor, the routine operations are already in place. Their challenge lies in understanding which processes they need to change, and which ones to leave alone.

The agricultural process is circular. Each cycle ends with the beginning of the next cycle. Improvements are incremental. A farmer may think up a new way to plow, but experimenting with a plowing technique while changing the irrigation levels and shifting the planting times carries too much risk of failure.

Most entrepreneurs concentrate on achieving an objective. There is always a new sales goal, a new territory, or a new customer to land. They frequently forget about the second half of the circle, the time after the harvest when their farmers need to prepare for the next cycle. Farmers assess the last season's results in order to know what changes need to be made and why. Hunters introduce new techniques on the fly. They don't know if an idea will work until they try it. Farmers need more assurance than that.

This is where the management tools of goal setting and performance reviews enter the picture. If you are a typical hunter, you probably wince internally at the performance review process. Entrepreneurs look ahead. We seldom dwell on the past, or at least not for very long. Just thinking about setting aside valuable time for structured review and measurement with the farmers gives many hunters the screaming meemies.

Managing farmers is more than just telling them *what* to do. It involves helping them understand *why* they should do it, and the benefits of doing it right. Just because I am referring to the majority of employees as farmers, please don't slide into the prejudice that they are somehow inferior to hunters or require less motivation. These aren't the human automatons of Fritz Lang's *Metropolis*. Farmers work in their own self-interest as much as any hunter does.

There is a very old cartoon about performance reviews. (It is so old that I first received it via fax machine.) It gives tongue-in-cheek instructions on how to conduct an employee review. Begin by scheduling it as late in the day as possible, so that it infringes on the employee's personal time. Make sure to mention several times how you hate the process, and wish you didn't need to engage in it at all. Be certain that you find things to criticize, preferably the employee's personal habits. Compare the employee to co-workers whom you think do a better job. Always finish by saying that the employee is a valued contributor, and you hope that he will perform even better in the future.

Does that sound like any reviews you remember? Humor is seldom funny because it is unrecognizable; it is funny because it's so familiar.

Another kind of performance evaluation is every bit as familiar. It's where the reviewer avoids any constructive criticism, glosses over any goals, and closes with a wage change announcement. The employee receives about a four ("meets or exceeds expectations") on a scale of five, learns nothing, and shuffles back to his daily responsibilities.

Think of the *Peanuts* cartoons where Charlie Brown is being harangued by his teacher. The employee hears *"Wah, wah, wah, wah, wah,* satisfactory, *wah, wah, wah, wah, wah,* improvement, *wah,wah,* 10% or $1.42 per hour, *wah,wah ..."* If you are including wage changes in your performance review discussion, stop it. The employee is only listening for the number, and remembers *nothing else* once it is announced. Try to keep salary adjustments and reviews at least a few months apart from each other.

Like it or not, entrepreneurs must be communicators in order to be successful. Their abhorrence of this one, critical form of communication often leads them to build layer upon layer of alternative mechanisms that take more time, more energy, and fail to accomplish the vital objective of actually motivating employees. In an entrepreneurial organization, you improve performance by *talking* to your employees.

A logical, sensible, and human employee evaluation system is really an entrepreneur's dream. You don't have to go through complicated metrics. After all, you are only interested in whether the employee is doing a better job than the last time you spoke. Evaluations aren't for meting out discipline. Waiting for a review so that you can point out failure is cowardice.

BakerRisk is an engineering company with about 160 employees in seven offices on both sides of the Atlantic. Employees receive written evaluations annually. The company puts a high value on culture, so much so that they fly in all employees for an annual meeting while the review process is going on. They don't present the reviews during that meeting, however. The focus is on company goals and objectives. Individual goal setting and coaching is done on the office or department level.

As engineers, you might expect them to have a very structured review process, and they do. The attention to detail is in making sure the approaches and scoring are consistent between offices and departments. The review itself is deceptively simple.

> Performance reviews are about accountability, not measurement

Employees are evaluated in three areas: individual performance (teamwork, external customer focus, internal customer focus, and communication), personal skills (job knowledge, personal development, and problem solving) and effectiveness (accountability, work quality/quantity, planning, conduct, and fiscal awareness).

Each employee first rates him or herself. The immediate supervisor then rates them using the same form, with differences discussed and passed to the top of the company if there are any disagreements. Then the employee and the company agree on goals for the coming year.

Note that although you might expect engineers to focus on tangible metrics, eleven of the twelve rated areas are subjective, behavioral tendencies. It's actually a brilliant approach. Most companies weight about 80% of their hiring decisions on skills, and make about 80% of their terminations based on behavior. BakerRisk only hires qualified engineers with proven skills. Whether or not they succeed depends on their behavioral characteristics.

Think about it. How many times have you hired an administrative employee to do data entry or word processing, and then terminated them because they couldn't type? Probably very few. How about terminations for poor accuracy, tardiness, absenteeism, or inability to follow instructions? Those are behavioral terminations.

Why then would you evaluate an employee based on his skills? You evaluate based on his behavior. The best way to do that is by discussing it, not by trying to shoehorn their behavior into specious skills measurements.

This doesn't mean that metrics don't matter. In the ten years through 2004, BakerRisk grew by about 50%. That year, they realized relatively poor utilization (billable hour per engineer) and profitability slipped. For the first time, they instituted measurements of contract backlogs, and began managing business development and recruiting according to those backlog measurements. They rated employees not by whether they did their assigned work correctly, but by how much they reached out to others in the organization to seek additional assignments. The company grew by *300%* in the next eight years.

The difference was accountability, not measurement. "Manage what you measure" can be misleading. You measure the results that you want, but you manage the *behaviors* that create the results. As BakerRisk discovered, the difference is profound.

Before we move on from the painful subject of evaluations, a moment for a word on employee self-appraisals. Many business owners fear the self-appraisal process because they think employees will use it as a negotiating ploy. They believe employees will build a case based on over-estimating their abilities and contributions in anticipation of the boss trying to counter with criticisms, and a hope that the two can negotiate a compromise (usually a pay increase), that is somewhere in between.

That is almost never the case when evaluations are fair, and compensation increases are separate from the review. In our company, we make it plain that wage increases are dependent on a number of things including performance, but also taking into consideration other factors outside the employee's control. Company profitability, market conditions, and the cost of expenses and benefits in general (say, for fuel or health insurance) are all influential in determining how much we can afford to pay someone.

Pretending that the employees' performance is the *only* factor in how much they can earn is misleading and unfair. Our business does not operate in a vacuum, and we don't pretend that our employees do either.

The farming cycle for an employee must come full circle. Unlike hunters, farmers don't move forward in a straight line, always thinking about the next objective. They need to do a job, review it, decide or learn what could be incrementally changed for improvement, and then start again. That requires management.

An entrepreneur's success is largely a result of his ability to communicate a vision and direction to customers and employees. Performance metrics and reports don't do that very well. If you are trying to utilize big organizations' measurements to influence your employees, save yourself a lot of time and trouble and talk to them instead. That is leadership.

Empowerment

We can't leave the discussion of dealing with farmers without talking a bit more about empowerment. The medical assistant story was an unfortunate outcome of an empowerment initiative, but there are benefits that we haven't yet discussed.

Entrepreneurs often make the mistake of believing that empowering employees means treating the farmers as if they were hunters. Using the old axiom of, "Treat others the way you would want to be treated," seems to encourage unlimited delegation (not abdication!) of authority, and the flexibility to be creative in problem solving and solutions.

That way lays madness. *You* make your decisions tempered by the knowledge that a negative result is entirely yours to absorb or fix. Employees don't share the same level of responsibility, and therefore, should not enjoy the same level of authority.

As my friend Larry Linne, the author of *Make the Noise Go Away* says, "A mistake may be the employee's responsibility, but it will always remain your consequence."

In an entrepreneurial organization, empowerment isn't a result of delegating as much as it is communication. Leading hunters depends on your ability to communicate your *vision*. Managing farmers depends on your ability to communicate your *expectations*. Empowering employees is a result of your ability to communicate *objectives*.

For employees to completely understand how to make decisions, they have to understand what they are trying to accomplish. Too often, we try to "dumb down" their responsibilities in simplistic terms. We relate only the operational outcome we seek, not the bigger picture of *why* that outcome is desirable. Understanding the reasoning behind the objective allows them to consider solutions that may not occur to you.

 Empowerment comes by communicating objectives

The owner of a temporary staffing company recently presented me with a problem. He had a supervisor who was responsible for dispatching staff from one of his company's locations. The assignments were often day-to-day or week-to-week.

The dilemma was how to handle the supervisor's ongoing failure to complete the reports necessary for billing and legal compliance. She was frequently out of the office, filling in for one or another employee who had failed to report for that day's assignment. When told that she should not be filling in for entry-level staff, she responded, "You said that the most important thing in our company was excellent customer service. If I hadn't filled in, the customer would have been left short-handed."

What followed was a typical exchange between a hunter/owner and a farmer/employee:

"Why didn't you call in some additional staff?"
"No one would work on short notice for $10 an hour."
"Why didn't you offer $12, or even $15, an hour?"
"Because we budgeted the work based on $10 an hour."
"You make $24 an hour."
"I am already included in the budget. We don't incur any additional expense if I go."

"But we don't get the billing or compliance paperwork done."

"My bonus depends on keeping to the budget."

"The budget is meaningless if we can't bill the customer."

"I thought our priority was excellent customer service."

Does this sound familiar? This isn't a discussion about the job objectives. The employee changed arguments three times in this short exchange, from customer satisfaction to budgeted pay rates to the bonus incentive program and back to customer service. Each time she was claiming to do what her boss said was most important.

The owner is playing catch-up with these serial arguments because his view of the situation is holistic, considering all the variables at the same time. The customer must be served, the company must maintain its reputation for dependability, the required reports must be generated, and it has to all be accomplished while maintaining profitability.

He is seeking a solution that satisfies all the requirements *given the situation and resources available.* She is trying to follow rules. When following one rule appears to conflict with another, she chooses the one that is more convenient or more readily available, rather than trying to reach a balance between the two.

Employees can only make decisions based on the information they are given. If all they have are rules, then no matter how dedicated and well intentioned they are, they will make decisions according to the rules. When they understand that the company runs according to a multi-faceted set of objectives, they are better able to comprehend the juggling that good decision making requires.

Empowerment is a process whereby employees are free to bend the rules in order to achieve an objective. Usually the solution to a problem involves compromise. In the staffing company, the solution required balancing between profit, customer satisfaction, and legally required paperwork.

Farmers will ask for a clear set of rules. Empowering employees means teaching them that the answers aren't necessarily the same every time. The staffing supervisor should fill in personally in some situations. In others, she might decide to take a hit on profitability or even explain to a customer why the company can't fill the job that day. If the owner dictated that any one factor was always paramount, he would probably face unsatisfactory solutions two-thirds of the time.

Hunters expect to deal with multiple variables. Farmers prefer working on one thing at a time. If rules were infallible, there would not be a problem in the first place. Employees have to learn that problems are not unusual. They are expected, and solving them is everyone's job. Empowering them to solve problems requires their understanding of the company's larger objectives.

Focusing on objectives includes an understanding of how money is made and what profits are used for. That is sometimes difficult for employees and, surprisingly, for business owners as well. We will look at your attitude toward profit, and how it affects your employees, in the next chapter.

Hunters consider multiple variables in their decisions

Chapter 10
Dealing with Yourself

"We have met the enemy and he is us."— Pogo

LIKE MOST POPULAR APHORISMS, Pogo's insight into human nature is ubiquitous because it is so painfully true. The hunting traits that make entrepreneurs successful in surmounting challenges that would defeat most people are the same traits that often keep them from growing beyond a modest level of success.

Starting a business is easy. Making it successful is hard work. Building it to the point where it is financially successful and isn't hard work is a challenge that the majority of small business owners never overcome.

Doug Tatum, the founder of Tatum CFO in Atlanta, describes the conditions that plague many owners in his book *No Man's Land*. An entrepreneur starts an enterprise. Through hard work and long hours, he builds the company to a point where he is making three times what he would if working as an employee. Unfortunately, he is also doing the work of three employees to do it.

There are a number of reasons why an entrepreneur gets stuck in no man's land. He may lack the experience to develop systems. He might be protective of the technical prowess that he used to start the business. He could be reluctant to teach others how to deliver his products and services in a way he finds acceptable. For many entrepreneurs I know, the real reason is that they prefer chaos.

 Real success is owning a business that isn't hard work

Thriving on Chaos

Hunters have always dealt with uncertainty. When a farmer wakes up in the morning, he knows where the field is. He knows which crop he has planted. He knows the tasks that need to be done that day. He knows, at least in general terms, how much work is required to be successful.

The hunter enjoys none of this predictability. He doesn't know where he is going to find game, or whether he will find any at all. It may be right outside his door, or he may spend hours tracking, with no guarantee of results. When the opportunity for a kill presents itself, he might miss and all of his efforts will be wasted. He may return empty-handed, leaving only greater pressure to be successful the next day, but with no improvement in his chances for a favorable outcome.

Hunters thrive on this uncertainty. They know it's what makes them different from farmers. They can make critical decisions based on incomplete information. They trust their instincts. They persevere in a chosen course of action because they are confident that their skills will eventually triumph, even if the odds are against them.

When a hunter is successful, the organization grows. In a cruel paradox, the more successful he is, the more the resulting enterprise looks like farming. The hunter tries to become a farmer. The entrepreneur tries to become a manager.

The tenacious problem solving approach to building a business doesn't work the same way when you are managing an organization of farmer employees. Farmers don't respond well to an atmosphere of constant uncertainty.

The owner of a local auto parts wholesaler identifies a problem. Customers are complaining about late delivery times on the daily routes. He announces that from now on, all trucks must be fully loaded a half hour before their scheduled departure. This will allow the drivers to plan their routes and organize their paperwork before going on the road.

The salespeople (hunters) concentrate on increasing sales. They ask, "Has the truck left yet?" When told it is loaded, but still on-premises, they produce one last minute order, inevitably for a new customer, or for a customer who desperately needs the merchandise that day.

The owner tries assigning a stand-by order picker in the warehouse for these last-minute calls. He moves up the "hard" deadline for orders, but the salespeople are swamped with calls near cut off time, so he tasks an assistant to help with order processing during the last hour before the delivery runs leave. When that bogs down, he starts flagging certain customer's orders for processing without approval from the credit department.

Now the owner has changed the ordering process, shifted the time frames when the customers can call, re-tasked two employees, and implemented a credit process that differs customer by customer. Each morning is still chaotic. The deliveries, not surprisingly, are still late.

Serial problem solving is rarely the way to fix a system. It's like taping a hole in a garden hose. The water leaks under the edge of the tape, so you add more. In a short time, you have two feet of tape around one small hole, and the hose still leaks.

Hunters have to make quick decisions. For entrepreneurs, the freedom to make those decisions is a driving force in their desire to own a business. They equate the ability to make decisions with control, and they are self-employed because they want control. If control is good, then making decisions must be good.

In the chaos of daily operations, making a decision, sometimes *any* decision, becomes an expression of the entrepreneur's ability to get things done. There is a feeling of satisfaction when people come to you for answers, and  then execute your commands. Those little adrenalin boosts, the rush that comes when you do something only you can do, becomes an addiction that gets you through the day.

The entrepreneur becomes the decision-maker-in-chief. Big decisions, small decisions, buying decisions, selling decisions, hiring decisions, disagreements among employees, customer requests; no decision escapes the input of the owner. He is the heroic central figure in the company's performance, standing high above the crowd, dispensing his critical wisdom.

If you are dispensing all the wisdom in your business, it can only grow as fast as you can make decisions; and you are only one person. The first step in transitioning from an entrepreneurship to a managed organization is to break your own addiction to decision making.

Work Ethic

Most entrepreneurs credit their success to working very hard. Those who began as Technicians or Creators often came from an employed environment where they were top performers, but Inheritors and Acquirers frequently share those high performance characteristics.

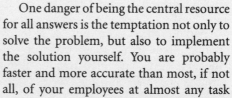

A decision-maker-in-chief limits the business

One danger of being the central resource for all answers is the temptation not only to solve the problem, but also to implement the solution yourself. You are probably faster and more accurate than most, if not all, of your employees at almost any task the business requires. Some business owners stop doing the technical work of the business only after other executive duties dominate their time, eroding their technical skills.

Maintaining a central role in your business makes it difficult to rely on anyone else in your absence. It leads to a business where you have to be available for every moment of operation. Business owners who follow the "first one to arrive, last to leave" approach to running their companies do it for one or more of the following reasons:

- They don't trust their employees to be productive without oversight.
- They have too much to do, even when working longer hours than anyone else.
- They don't allow anyone else to make decisions when they are not there.
- They feel the need to set an example.

- They feel guilty about letting others work to make them money unless they are working too.

The first three reasons are management issues and are addressed by getting the people or the systems (and preferably both), in place to allow the farmers to understand what they need to be doing on a day-to-day basis.

Let's focus on feeling that you must set an example. Is part of your leadership responsibility setting the standard for work ethic?

How do your employees know whether you are working hard? If you think it is because you take more orders or box more widgets than anyone else, you are setting an example; but your business will suffer.

If you think they consider you an example because you are there all the time, you are deluding yourself. Once you've fixed the "Only I can make any decision" problem, the need for you to be present as a constant example goes away.

My friend Kevin Armstrong, a former schoolteacher and now a very successful coach and consultant in Vancouver, British Columbia, says a business owner has two, and only two, responsibilities to the company.

The first responsibility is to get the right people in the right jobs doing the right things. It is no small task, but any owner will agree that it is the key to success.

The second job of a business owner is to have a few new ideas each month. There is no earthly reason to be in the office to have an idea. In fact, you probably have better ideas when you are somewhere else, like lying on a beach in Cuba. (Kevin is Canadian. They like to go to Cuba for a cheap island vacation.)

Remember, giving someone an answer isn't the same as having an idea. An idea is new, something that changes how other people work, not merely fixes what they are doing wrong.

A business owner has two, and only two, responsibilities

John Kruger owns Nevada Brake and Auto Parts in Las Vegas. (He is not the parts wholesaler described previously.) A former Apple Executive in Atlanta, John was an Acquirer, purchasing the nine-year-old company from its retiring founder in 1985. John moved to Las Vegas, and began running day-to-day operations of the company. He opened additional locations, streamlined the operations, and acted as NBA's high-level salesman to the major accounts in the city.

Nevertheless, John wasn't enamored with living in the desert. His friends and interests remained in Atlanta, as did a home he kept there. He began traveling back to Georgia whenever he could spare the time. After a few years, he found himself living in Atlanta again, and traveling to Las Vegas to work in the business as needed.

John built a solid team of managers. He participated in major decisions, such as taking on a new line of products, by phone. He would hop on an airplane if needed for a critical meeting, but as time wore on the interval between those trips stretched from weeks to months.

John maintained this lifestyle for almost twenty years, during which Nevada Brake & Auto grew, prospered, and made him a lot of money. His ideas continued to improve the business, and even earned it a write-up for innovation in *Entrepreneur* magazine.

However, no entrepreneur is ever completely free from the risks and responsibilities of owning the business. In 2007, Las Vegas was the worst hit market in the United States when the subprime mortgage market collapsed. John had to move back to Nevada to take the reins of his struggling company. On a positive note, he found that spectacular condominiums could be had for very, very cheap rents.

John replaced the general manager, stabilized the business, restored profitability, and began again planning his eventual departure from Las Vegas. This time he decided that his exit from the company was the best way to make sure he didn't have to return.

The employees of Nevada Brake & Auto Parts didn't resent John's lifestyle. He was the owner, and his lifestyle was his choice. They did their jobs each day, selling, delivering, collecting money, and ordering replacement stock. They made bank deposits and paid the bills. Until a major external change created challenges beyond the scope of their experience, they ran the daily business operations effectively and efficiently.

John came up with new ideas. Sometimes he could relay them to his managers, but occasionally he had to fly to Las Vegas to implement them personally. How and when he did that was his choice. The variability of his schedule discouraged the employees from running the company differently when the boss was out of town.

Giving someone an answer isn't the same as having an idea

In reality, few entrepreneurial success stories are perfect, but most owners I know would gladly take *two decades* of limited, absentee working hours as a part of their career.

Outproducing Your Employees

San Antonio, Texas is an unusual market. Now the seventh largest city in the U.S., it was largely a sleepy regional cattle and agricultural center until the advent of air conditioning and air travel. As such, it has incubated a disproportionate number of homegrown companies that are local market leaders in their industries.

The public accounting business was no different. In 2005, the *San Antonio Business Journal* listed the top CPA firms in the city by size. Of the ten largest firms, two were national, and all of the rest were one-office local businesses. These local firms ranged from fifteen to eighty-five professionals, with only two managed by a partner other than the original founder.

Outworking everyone else is an especially common cultural problem for the owners of professional firms where employee value is calculated in billable hours. Insurance brokers, accountants, engineers, physicians, architects, and attorneys frequently suffer from the high producer syndrome.

As with many other professional firms, the founders of these practices were ambitious technicians, previously employed by the

"Big Eight." (For younger readers, there was a very long period of time when eight national firms dominated accounting for large organizations. The financial markets, mergers, and regulators have reduced that number to only four today.)

The entrepreneurial ability of these founders to attract and retain clients brought in more work than they could handle. Each had reached a point where he felt constrained by the pace of the partner track in a large firm, and decided that he could be wealthier faster on his own.

Most of these eight local firms assumed a similar business model. The founders (typically two or three partners) brought in business and maintained the major client relationships. They hired other accountants to do the daily technical work. The farmers they hired were certainly competent and capable professionals; they just weren't hunters. The founders did all the hunting while the farmers cultivated and delivered, and their firms prospered.

> Hunters can't lead by outworking everyone else

As business grew, the founders recognized the best farmers by making them partners. To free up their time for hunting new clients, they handed off work that was lower margin, or where the client relationship only needed maintenance. In every case, the founding partners continued to manage the largest portfolio of clients in the company.

As the founders aged, they began looking at the issue of succession. To their surprise, there were no hunters who could assume their roles! They had backfilled their organizations with farmers, none groomed to assume the duties of rainmaker or "face of the firm."

Most professional firms take their profits beyond necessary working capital and distribute them each year. Retirement benefits are usually unfunded. That means that there isn't any pool of money to secure future payments as in a 401K or similar defined contribution plan. The viability of these partners' retirement plans depended on the continued existence of a profitable firm, which had to generate sufficient cash flow to pay the current partners as well as the retirees.

Here is what happened to the eight local firms between the years 2006 and 2011.

At the first practice, two of the founding partners retired, leaving the third founder to run it alone. He quickly sold it to a regional firm from outside the market.

At both the second and third practices, one of two founding partners retired, leaving the other to merge with a regional firm. In these two cases, the acquirers paid no cash, agreeing only to assume the pension liabilities for retired partners.

At the fourth practice, one founder retired, but the other was determined to maintain the firm's independence. He offered the managing partner position to a senior partner, who turned it down. Then it was offered to a younger partner, who also turned it down. Both said that they had plenty of work and a satisfactory income. They expressly refused to add business development to their responsibilities. They were farmers.

This founder searched outside the company and brought in another accountant as a managing partner in training. He failed. Ultimately, they merged with a regional firm much like the two discussed above.

At the fifth practice, the farmers had grown old with the partners. Finally, they were facing a near-term situation that would have left three partners responsible for generating the cash flow to pay themselves, and at the same time fund five other partners' retirement incomes. They merged with a national firm. Again, they based the purchase price on an assumption of the retirement liabilities.

At the sixth, one of the three founding partners retired, but two remain running the business. They are roughly the same size as they were ten years ago.

At the seventh, the founder, now well into his seventies, continues to lead the firm. He still manages many of the principle client contacts. At least one other partner has assumed, and then surrendered, the managing partner role. At this time their succession plan is unclear, or at least it hasn't been made public.

All seven of these firms were fortunate. San Antonio is a rapidly growing market that shrugged off much of the Great Recession. The absence of regional players in the market made the local firms prime acquisition candidates. Nonetheless, even such strategic positioning was not enough to command a price premium.

The eighth firm, Padgett, Stratemann & Company (PS&Co), doubled during the same period to nearly 250 professionals, almost five times the size of their closest independent competitor. The firm is named annually to the Top 100 Independent Accounting Firms in America, and is listed year after year in the local "Best Places to Work," employee surveys.

Developing hunters should start on the day of hire

The third generation managing partner of PS&Co. is John Wright. In his early forties, John fits few people's preconceived ideas of what a successful leader of a CPA firm should be. He is outgoing and loves nothing better than to take a client hunting. He makes it plain to everyone that he would much rather be at his ranch than working in the office. He's also vocal about his belief that everyone else in the firm should have some interest that they enjoy a lot more than accounting.

John has virtually no direct client account responsibility and no personal target for billable hours. His job is solely to manage the firm. How did PS&Co. reach this level of performance *and* develop a culture of work/life balance at the same time?

For years, Padgett Stratemann has done things that most accounting firms say they do, but few really implement. They focus on developing the next generation of hunters, beginning almost as soon as someone joins the firm.

In most firms, a new graduate or accountant who has recently passed the CPA examination is treated as a farmer's farmer. They are worker bees, poring through financial records at an audit or cranking out tax returns. In Padgett Stratemann, those employees have goals that involve much more than billable hours and continuing education. Young associates enroll in Toastmasters® groups. They join business associations and are expected to become active and valued leaders in those organizations. As they progress, the firm often hires executive coaches to work with them, and part of their goal setting includes the development of newer associates under them.

Most importantly, *a professional cannot ignore his development goals simply by generating billable hours.* In every other CPA firm I know, the partners are willing to overlook almost everything else if an associate is putting substantial sums in the partners' pockets. At Padgett Stratemann, just being a human billing machine is not enough.

John thrived in that environment. He is a hunter, both literally and figuratively. He reminisces about how, as a young accountant, his supervisors would agonize over his annual work budgets. John would always delegate a substantial portion of the work he had done the year before, and budget his time for 25% less than his minimum billing goal. "I'll make it," John would say. "If I don't have capacity, how will I find the time to generate new business?"

Of course, not every accountant at PS&Co. is a born hunter. Some can be trained to do a bit of hunting, and some are certainly valued for their technical prowess. If you refuse to hunt at all, however, you won't be a partner there.

The most successful independent firm in the city got that way by being the one that *wasn't* focused solely on a production-based work ethic.

Where's Waldo?

If you've raised children in the last twenty-five years or so, you have probably played a version of *Where's Waldo?* The books teach children about different cultures and geography by having them examine pictures to find a bespectacled character in a striped shirt.

Many entrepreneurs believe that their employees are playing *Where's Waldo?* every time the owner is out of the office.

For most owners, the business consumes so much of their time that they have little guilt about personal tasks handled during business hours. They check investments and bank balances on the Internet (often in violation of their own workplace policies). They stop to pick up dry cleaning or get a haircut in between appointments. That is fair, and it is small enough reward in relation to the total commitment their companies require.

Yet many owners worry about the message they are sending to employees when they are absent. "Do they think I'm home watching television?" "Do they know that I'm in a long business meeting, trying to land a customer whose business will pay their salaries for a month?" An owner's concern about the business can become paranoia about sending the right message, and setting the example for employees to follow.

In reality, most employees are more concerned about doing their jobs than where *you* are at every moment. When I call a business and ask for the owner, the answer is frequently "He's not here right now." In such cases I will ask (for both of our convenience), "Do you know when he will be back?" Unless I am speaking with the boss's assistant, the response is usually negative. The employees do not know where he (or she) is, what he is doing, or when he will return. When you are gone, you are gone. When you are there, you are there. No one is judging your activity but you.

You might be playing golf, but perhaps it is with a key vendor. You might be calling on a customer, buying a new piece of equipment, or attending your kid's school play. The employees don't know, and they usually don't think about it much. You are the boss and if you are a good leader, the employees naturally assume that you are doing something that you are supposed to be doing.

If you don't have anything to do, don't go to the office! You can do a lot more damage when you are idle at work than if you are idle at home. What if an employee stops by your office and finds you playing computer games? What would be worse, employees who suspect that you are doing nothing when you are absent, or ones who are *sure* you are doing nothing useful when you are there?

There is one exception to making your own hours that I coach against — coming in late every day. I believe that it creates several problems. Chronic lateness is a punishable offense in all but the most relaxed organizations. It is by definition "bad behavior" that engenders disciplinary action. When the boss shows up every day an hour or two after work begins for everyone else, the employees naturally assume that he was just sleeping in.

Most importantly, a boss who consistently begins work an hour or more after the employees effectively creates a second starting time for each day. The 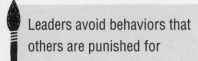 first hour becomes "ramp up" time. Everyone can get a second cup of coffee, discuss the previous night's ball game, and send someone out for breakfast. The real work usually does not begin in earnest until the boss arrives.

If you have ten employees, the unproductive cost of a collective lost hour each morning equals a full-time employee each week. That is a high price to pay for your morning flexibility. How much more would you have to accomplish in order to support a full time employee who does nothing?

Control over your time is a privilege of ownership. If you are going to be out of the office for an hour or a day, it has much less impact than you might fear. Just make sure that it isn't when everyone else in the company can build it into their work schedule.

Other than regularly coming in late, an employer's absence rarely leads to a game of *Where's Waldo?*

Profit Guilt

The last reason some business owners follow the "first to arrive; last to leave" approach to running their companies is profit guilt. They feel uncomfortable about letting others work to make them money unless they are working too.

Before you decide I'm crazy and throw my book away (there's a lot of good stuff still to come), that statement probably should be qualified.

What do *you* think is *a lot* of money?

Leaders avoid behaviors that others are punished for

In his 1943 paper, *A Theory of Human Motivation*, psychologist Abraham Maslow postulated his hierarchy of needs. Today, it is a widely accepted description of what drives people. It is clearly valid when we are discussing entrepreneurial attitudes toward profits.

Level One: Physiological (food, clothing, shelter) When I ask a newly minted entrepreneur, one who is in the first stages of building his company, what his objective is, the answer is usually, "I want to make a decent living and provide for my family."

Level Two: Safety (security of body and family) This is exactly what entrepreneurs who have made it past basic survival say. They seek financial security for themselves and their loved ones.

Level Three: Belonging (friendship and family) In business, it's being able to run with the pack. You want to enjoy the same benefits as others who are your business peers. This might mean a motorcycle, a second home, or season tickets for a local pro team.

Level Four: Esteem (confidence, achievement, the respect of others) For business owners, it is the recognition that comes with success. It is having enough income to donate to a school or church, or joining a country club.

Level Five: Self-actualization (creativity, spontaneity, problem solving) Level Five is where *all bets are off*. Only *you* can decide what constitutes a "fair" return on your work. For many owners, that decision becomes self-limiting. How much should you make? Is it merely more than any other employee in your business makes? Is it twice as much? Ten times as much? A hundred times?

Edward Deming, the guru of Total Quality Management, said that no CEO should make more than fifty times what the lowest paid employee makes. If an entry-level worker is paid $10 an hour, that means the business owner should make no more than $500 an hour or $20,000 for a forty-hour week. Many entrepreneurs work far more than forty hours a week, and most do not make $1,000,000 a year.

Large publicly traded companies long ago abandoned Deming's compensation guidelines, but the typical entrepreneur has some distance to go before this becomes a problem.

What amount of money would let you "have it all"? Do you want a second home or a bigger boat? Does your definition of success include world travel or philanthropy? Do you want to have a building or perhaps even an entire school named after you?

Entrepreneurs who limit themselves to the first four levels of motivation are restricting their company's success. They stop hunting and begin farming to maintain a level where they feel comfortable.

Assuming you pay your employees fairly for their work, if you are afraid to let them know how much you make because you think they will judge you, then you have profit guilt. It is your business, and *you have the right to make as much money as you can.* Your employees share little of your risk.

I know very few successful entrepreneurs who hoard their profits. Those who reach Level Five use some, and sometimes most of the money they make to help others. That is their choice, but first they had to make the money. No one benefits from throttling back the potential of a business in a misguided attempt to be "fair."

Equally important, don't try to downplay the money you make to your employees. They won't believe you anyway. We once did a survey of two companies. One was a technology

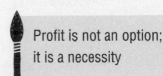

Profit is not an option; it is a necessity

firm, where most of the employees had master's degrees or better. The other employed laborers, many of whom spoke little English.

We asked both employee groups the same question. "Of every dollar this company charges for its work, how much do you think winds up in the pocket of the owners?"

In both organizations, the answer was the same: fifty percent.

Telling your employees that you don't really make any money only generates disbelief. Every time you buy a new car or go away on vacation, they are crediting it to the fact that you are rich. You might as well learn to live with it, and make it the truth.

Besides, no one wants to work for a loser.

Chapter 11
Hiring isn't Adoption

CRINGE WHEN A BUSINESS OWNER tells me, "Our company is just like a family." I have a family, and my business is *nothing* like that.

Unfortunately, many businesses *do* run like families. One employee is like weird old Uncle Bob, who is only seen at weddings and funerals, and happily left to himself the rest of the time. Another fills the role of notorious cousin Jane, whose relationship disasters provide ample grist for the gossip mill.

Family members have the right to unconditional love. They can make mistakes (and in the case of children, the same mistake multiple times) and expect to be forgiven every time. What they receive is based on need, not ability.

If that is how you treat your employees, I am betting that your business is in big trouble.

Employees are hired. They have a contract, whether it is written or verbal. That agreement sets expectations for a certain level of job performance, in return for which they receive wages and benefits. If they can't (or won't) hold up their end of the bargain, you have no obligation to stick to yours.

More importantly, allowing one employee to fail without suffering the consequences is unfair to all the others. If you regularly make exceptions for poor performers, you won't have any good employees left to do the important stuff.

When you interview a new employee, I am sure you say things like, "We want people on our team whom we can depend on." or, "You will be joining a group of folks who all work hard and do a great job." Do you *believe* it when you say it? I hope so, or else I know where to place the blame for performance problems.

Patrick Lencione says that the most neglected role of a CEO is communicating bad news to subordinates; no one wants to be the bad guy.

Owners make many excuses for hanging on to an underperformer. He does the job well enough. Her mistakes are regular but usually minor. He was ill for a long time and has never quite gotten back up to speed. She has family issues and is distracted.

Employees have lives. They fall in love, break up, get back together, get married, and get divorced. They have children, parents, siblings, and pets. They buy houses, make investments both good and bad, and get sick. The vagaries of life events aren't sufficient reason to pay someone not to do a job.

Naturally, we all care about our employees and want to treat them well, but not at the expense of running a successful enterprise. Do you think I sound too callous? Try this little exercise. Call your employees together and make this speech.

"As some of you know, I have had a number of personal problems over the last few months. Things aren't so good at home, and my portfolio has taken a shellacking. I've also been to see the doctor, and he says that I have a chronic condition that, while not life-threatening, will require some extensive treatment."

"Because of these issues I haven't been able to give my full attention to the business, and our performance has suffered as a result. I am fully confident that we will recover, but in the meantime we won't be able to issue paychecks until further notice."

Yeah. You know how much sympathy you would get. Probably the best you could hope for is a mumbled, "I'm sorry," as your longest-tenured employee cleans out his desk.

Entrepreneurs enjoy less slack, less margin for error, and less flexibility than their employees. Expecting a reasonable day's work for a reasonable day's pay is fair, equitable, and sustainable. Paying for work you don't receive is unfair to you, your customers, and your other employees.

On the other hand, as an owner you can do things for people that others can't. You can make exceptions. For example, I know an owner who is allowing an employee to use a company vehicle in violation of written policy.

I know what you've been told. If you do it for one person, you have to do it for everyone. That's not exactly true. This owner discovered that an employee had a child who was critically ill and receiving 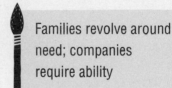 care in a specialty hospital in another city. The employee's car was undependable, and because of that, he was unable to drive across the state on weekends to visit his sick son.

> Families revolve around need; companies require ability

The owner took the employee aside, and gave him the keys to a company pickup truck for weekend use. He told the worker to keep it quiet, but just a few weeks after he started lending out the vehicle, another employee approached him.

"Boss, I noticed that you've been letting Andy use a company truck on weekends. My car is in the shop and I have tickets to the big game upstate this weekend. I need to take one of our trucks to get there."

Here is how the owner replied.

"Chuck, you know that we have a policy forbidding the use of company vehicles for personal reasons. I have made a change in that policy. From now on, *any* employee with over ten years of service in our company, and who has a child undergoing life-saving treatment in another city, and is without other means to visit that child, will be permitted to use a company vehicle on weekends for that purpose."

Game, set, match. You make the rules, although labor law sometimes makes it a pain to live within them. If you are smart

An owner has the right
to make exceptions

enough to build a business, you should be smart enough to figure out how to help employees who deserve it. It's good to be king.

Paternalism

Most entrepreneurs are at least a bit paternalistic (or maternalistic, as the case may be). Russell Ackoff, one of the great organizational theorists, first observed the characteristics of a paternalistic organization. He described some of those characteristics as including:

- A values system that places emphasis on employee longevity over innovation

- A suspicion that outside influence is bad if it disagrees with what is "known" in the company

- A tendency to believe that the ideal response to any crisis or change is to make things return to the way they were before

These traits of paternalistic leaders are described in an article by Terri L. Bennink from the Columbia Leadership Institute:

- Paternalistic leaders are benevolent but intrusive. They believe that they know what is best for the company, and for those working in it.

- The paternalist uses his power to control, protect, punish, and reward in return for obedience and loyalty.

Note the last point well. Rewards are doled out in return for obedience and loyalty, not performance. If an organization values longevity over accomplishment, it has one foot in the grave of mediocrity.

There is a cliché that goes, *"Twenty years of experience can mean twenty years of experience, or it can be one year of experience repeated twenty times."* An entrepreneurial business grows because its people grow. If they are jogging in place, so is the company.

Running a paternalistic organization has other disadvantages. It requires a lot of your personal time and attention. It depends on your ongoing presence and involvement in all decisions, which, as previously discussed, limits your growth.

If your company is going to grow without your constant attention, you have to be a boss, not a parent.

Perhaps the toughest part about growing beyond paternalism is employee expectations. Farmer employees prefer clear direction and specific duties. In their life experience, direction usually came from their parents. It's easy for them to cast the boss in a familiar role. If you accept it, you are cheating yourself as much as you are them.

This is an appropriate time to discuss the influence of the media in your business. Regardless of how you treat your employees in the workplace, they go home to watch television every night. There, they see caricatures of employers. Bosses on TV are venal manipulators, idiots, or both.

From *Taxi* to *The Office* and from *Just Shoot Me* to *The Drew Carey Show*, bosses are portrayed as sneaky, self-centered, and interested only in how they can exploit their employees.

I believe that every employer has to work harder to gain employee trust because of the negative portrayals on television. No matter how honest your A boss has to overcome media stereotypes every day

motivation, when you say to an employee, "This is for your benefit," or "I want to help you," you are working against a lifetime of media brainwashing that causes him to think, at least for a second, "Oh yeah? I wonder what he *really* wants."

Whatever your management style, it has to be honest and real. Every owner is competing on a field tilted against him. Trust takes a long time to build, and getting caught in one falsehood can destroy an employee relationship forever.

Building trust is different from acceptance. Trust evolves when you are fair. It requires that you be consistent (or explain exceptions when they arise). Trust is an employee's understanding that if he holds up his end of the contract, you will hold up yours.

Paternalism violates that trust. Employees are rewarded outside the understanding of what the contract means (even if it is just by being paid for poor performance). Paternalism corrupts the relationships that lead to high performance in an organization.

Educating Employees

Whether you are working with hunters or farmers, every employee has the right to know how his or her work affects the company as a whole. The easiest (or perhaps the hardest) way to do this is by practicing *open book management.*

Before you groan, let me clarify a few common misconceptions. Open book management is about giving your employees visibility into how the business works. Visibility isn't transparency. They shouldn't know how *everything* works, or every detail of what you spend. In fact, sharing everything would probably make them panic.

Open book education isn't merely about sharing the numbers. It requires teaching employees about the need and uses for profit, and how it represents much more than money in the owner's pocket. Until your employees can comprehend some basic concepts of working capital, cash flow, reserves for emergencies, return on your investment, capital expenditures, and financing for growth, they are bound to misunderstand what "profit" really is.

Even the most well meaning attempts to teach employees about how the company makes money are fraught with risk. Sometimes, it is just too much information.

Cheryl Rickman owned Baker Surveying, a business with about twenty employees. After reading John Case's 1996 book *Open Book Management* she decided to educate her employees using his game show approach.

She invited her employees to a company wide meeting. As they entered, each employee was handed a sign designating a certain monthly expense, like "Office Rent: $4,500."

In the front of the room was a table piled high with "Baker Bucks," a $100 bill that she had duplicated on the copier. Cheryl started

Open book management offers visibility, not transparency

the meeting by announcing that the pile of bills represented one month's revenue for the business, or about $150,000. The employees were suitably impressed with the pile of 1,500 hundred-dollar bills.

Acting as the game show host, Cheryl began calling expenses from the audience, encouraging the employees to shout, "come on down!" as each was announced. Every employee counted out their expense amount from the pile on the table to considerable laughter and cheering.

When "Payroll" was called, the designated employee took about 50% of the revenue. The room began to get quiet as the employees regarded the much-smaller pile, and looked around for the remaining signs to see how many more expenses were left to pay.

By the time only "profit" remained on the table, the room had become silent. When Cheryl asked for questions, one of the administrative staff immediately raised her hand. "Are you trying to tell us that we are going out of business?"

Educating employees can be dangerous if it isn't handled correctly. They have to be told what they are seeing, not expected to figure it out for themselves. You may or may not want to discuss things like non-cash expenses. In Baker's case, for example, there was considerable depreciation for equipment and vehicles, so the cash flow was actually substantially more than the profits.

The most important concept in open book management education is return on investment. Your company, and the jobs you provide, exist because you invested in your business. If you are an Acquirer, it was probably cash or an assumption of debt. If you are an Inheritor, it may have been years of toiling for less pay than others, doing work for which you were overqualified, or perhaps paying on a note for the business over many years.

If you are a Technician or a Creator, you may have put in some money, but you certainly contributed effort and time, probably for a lot less return than you could have earned elsewhere. Sweat equity is a real cost.

Add up all of your investments, cash, reduced compensation, time, and anything else to which you can attach a reasonable number. (The total may shock you.) Then figure out your rightful return on your investment.

Many entrepreneurs do not understand profit

A traditional stock investment in a solid, publicly traded company might pay you between 6% and 8% a year in dividends and appreciation. At the other end of the ROI spectrum, investment bankers seek a potential return of 200% per year or more to make up for the risk of the many deals that pay back nothing.

In small business, the accepted risk-adjusted return for a private company is estimated at between 25% and 35% a year. That is what you should be making on your *investment* every year, not what you pay yourself in salary for the work you do. The amount that you fall short of that number each year, accumulates as part of your total investment.

That isn't profit. It is merely the risk-adjusted repayment of your costs. On top of that, you have to generate margins for reinvestment and growth. Only that which remains in *addition* to a return on investment, compensation for your work, reserves for unforeseen problems, and funding for expansion is really "profit."

Educating employees often brings with it education for the entrepreneur. Look at your business with the same criteria you would use to judge any other investment. Once you fully understand what you *should* be making from your business, it is a lot easier to get over any profit guilt from which you might be mistakenly suffering.

Sharing Decision Making

Many businesses that practice open book management also allow the employees to have a voice in some business decisions. While employee buy-in to a company's direction is a powerful alignment factor, it has to be handled carefully.

David Spencer founded OnBoard Software to provide upgrades and improvements to military aircraft. The company started in a surplus Air Force administration building, and to say that the surroundings were not luxurious would be charitable.

David was an avid disciple of open book management. Each month he would sit with his employees and go over each line item in the financial statements. (An aside: you NEVER share individual salaries.) His folks, mostly programmers, were smart, and could follow how their work flowed through to affect the bottom line.

OnBoard grew quickly and when it reached sixty employees, David decided to build a new headquarters. It was going to be every tech employee's dream. It was spacious and hip, with amenities ranging from an employee gym to the larger than life statue of British cartoon characters Wallace and Gromit in the lobby. (That is a long story for another time.)

Dave is a dedicated parent. He and his wife Jennifer have four sons, and he loves spending time with them. In designing his new building, David was devoted to the idea of incorporating a daycare center. He felt that providing a workplace where employees could be close to their kids would both make OnBoard more competitive in its recruiting, as well as bring in the type of people he wanted in his company.

As the construction got underway, the monthly financial review meetings with employees became more contentious. The childless employees wanted to know why profits were used on a facility they did not need and couldn't use. They suggested that David finance the daycare center out of his own pocket, or at least reverse the expenses from the company P&L before calculating their bonuses.

The childless employees also rejected David's recruiting argument. They saw themselves as top performers, and resented Sometimes, "open book" is too much information the implication that people with children were somehow more desirable.

In the end, David had to fall back on a diplomatic version of the ultimate argument. "It's my company, and if you don't like it you might have to go work somewhere else."

That is the final word. You built your company (despite any politician's claim to the contrary) and you have to decide what works best. If you are wrong, you, not your employees, are left holding the bag.

Parting Ways

Every employment relationship eventually ends. People in their twenties now expect to hold a lifetime average of 22 positions. Employees who spend their entire working life in one organization are so rare as to warrant newspaper stories at retirement.

> When you hire someone, the relationship will end in one of two ways

Practically speaking, when you hire an employee, there are only two ways the relationship can turn out: voluntary termination or involuntary termination. Few books on entrepreneurship talk about the pain of losing a great employee, but that's because we all like to live in our fantasy worlds.

Every day, when our good and valuable employees show up for work, we pretend that this is a day like all other days. As long as nothing goes wrong, tomorrow will be like today, and every day after that will be the same.

If we stopped to engage our powers of logic for a minute, we would realize that it isn't true. Even the best employees get other offers, or their spouses do. Lives change. People move on.

Hunters live with constant change, and the best anticipate future events. Being a successful business owner requires that you understand employee turnover, are prepared for it, and can get past it without losing momentum.

Voluntary Termination

Let's start with voluntary termination. I believe that, except in the rarest of situations, voluntary termination can be anticipated, planned, and accomplished with minimum pain for either the employee or the entrepreneur.

At each annual review, I ask the employee the same question with the same qualifier. "Where do you see yourself five years from now? By the way, 'somewhere else' is a perfectly acceptable answer."

Occasionally, the answer (either from dyed in the wool farmers or from someone who is trying to snow me) is, "I'd like to be right here, doing exactly this." More often, the employee expresses a desire for more money, greater responsibility or a different role. Sometimes we can accommodate those ambitions in our small company. Sometimes we can't.

Getting our eventual parting of the ways onto the table makes many employees nervous at first. Although *they* know that they won't be in this job forever, they are usually happy to let *you* wallow in your fantasy of perpetual stability.

Discussing an employee's ambitions honestly and openly has advantages for both parties. The employee is more comfortable and honest sharing his or her plans and timeframes. As an employer, I can help them work toward their goals. (We have a $1,000 annual use-it-or-lose-it self-improvement fund for each full-time worker. It is available specifically for developing skills that are *not* related to the business.)

My motivations aren't entirely altruistic. In return for understanding objectives, I get a loyal employee who will keep me apprised of his or her plans, and if they change, I have sufficient notice. When the time comes to move on, we can do it with plenty of warning, an orderly transition, and ample time to train a replacement.

Compare that to two weeks' notice, and the traditional scramble to recruit, interview, hire and train under a short deadline. It is no contest. Accept that all employees eventually leave, and start discussing that in a non-threatening way from their arrival. It's a far easier approach for all concerned.

Involuntary Termination

Many poor performers languish in place because the entrepreneur simply does not have the nerve to face them and say, "You're fired."

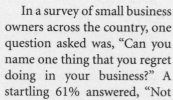

Check your responsibilities before deciding that an employee has failed

In a survey of small business owners across the country, one question asked was, "Can you name one thing that you regret doing in your business?" A startling 61% answered, "Not firing someone until long after I should have." Small businesses hire too fast and fire too slowly, when it should be the other way around.

Bad performers are a cancer. They corrupt the people around them. When you finally get up the gumption to let them go, other employees say, "What took you so long?"

Poor performance is not always the fault of the employee. When considering your options, take this simple self-test:

1. Did you develop a clear job description that fairly described what was expected?

2. Did you carefully screen for the necessary skills and behavioral traits when you hired?

3. Was the employee sufficiently trained for the job?

4. Did you create appropriate incentives to motivate the desired behavior?

5. Did you provide timely feedback and direction when performance was lacking?

If the answer is "yes" to all five questions, terminate the employee. If not, then you should step up, accept some responsibility for their failure, and correct your shortcomings as an employer before you make the employee pay the price.

Although laws and regulations have made termination a dicier proposition than ever before, you can't let that handcuff your ability to

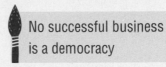

No successful business is a democracy

run the business as you wish. Most post-termination legal actions are for rules that were applied unevenly, or that weren't applied at all. If you are fair, if you give your hunters clear leadership and your farmers clear direction, you should be fine.

It's Good to be King

I try to hire the smartest people I can find and afford. I encourage them to use their intelligence to come up with alternative ways to do things. I ask their opinions, and have no problem with open disagreement. (Well, not *too* much.)

However, when a decision with company-wide implications has to be made, I am the one who makes it. More than once, a manager has come to me after an announcement for a conversation something like this:

Manager:	"I see you decided to move ahead with the new expansion plan."
Me:	"Yes, I think it is what we need to be doing."
Manager:	"I thought we talked about this."
Me:	"So we did."
Manager:	"I made it plain that I didn't think it was the right time."
Me:	"You were perfectly clear on that."
Manager:	"Then why did you do it anyway?"
Me:	"Because there is a difference between asking for your opinion and taking a vote. This isn't a democracy."

You didn't adopt your employees; you hired them. You should treat them as adults, and refuse to allow them to behave like children. A good boss respects the talents of his workers, educates them about the business, and solicits their ideas and opinions.

You remain the only one who carries the burden of ownership. You understand the risks, the rewards, the stress, the uncertainty, the liability, and the multiple potential consequences of every decision. That gives you the right to make them.

PART III: The Successful Hunter

Chapter 12
Defining Success

WHAT IS A SUCCESSFUL ENTREPRENEUR? The definition of "making it" in any small business is as individual as its owner. As a coach, I work with business owners to help them document their personal vision, an exercise to define making it in their own terms. Without a clear vision, the quest for growth and success can become a never-ending treadmill.

Many entrepreneurs achieve an enviable level of financial security, but find themselves working just as hard as when they were scrambling to eke out a paycheck. They continue to put in yeoman hours even after there is no longer the need. They chase ever-increasing profits long after accumulated wealth has secured their lifestyle.

Accomplishing your personal vision is not an end point, but it is a stopping point. It is a signpost to let you know that it's time to assess where you are, and where you are going.

John "Hutch" Hutcherson owned a successful local office of a national insurance and financial planning group. In his late sixties, Hutch remained healthy and very active. His success allowed him to spend considerable time on his chosen cause, prison ministry. Hutch's personal vision called for him to sell his business within two or three years, and then devote full time to his charitable work.

One day, Hutch excitedly presented an opportunity to his peer group in The Alternative Board®. A colleague in a nearby town was selling his business. Because of Hutch's success and impeccable reputation, the colleague wanted him to buy it. The business was healthy and the terms were extremely attractive. It would mean a sizeable leap in immediate income; and all the systems were in place to seamlessly assume the client base. Additionally, Hutch would be helping a long-time friend to realize his exit plan.

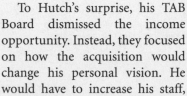

A personal vision is not an end point, but it is a stopping point

To Hutch's surprise, his TAB Board dismissed the income opportunity. Instead, they focused on how the acquisition would change his personal vision. He would have to increase his staff, as well as reduce the amount of time available for his ministry activities. A larger business would shift the field of potential buyers for his firm, and push back his possible exit by at least a few more years. Finally, the additional revenue would not dramatically change Hutch's lifestyle.

Hutch decided to pass on the deal. He happily executed his vision as planned, selling his business a couple of years later. Having his personal vision written down allowed him to judge an attractive short-term opportunity by its long-term impact. It was enough of a reminder to keep him on his chosen path.

Measuring Profit

As we discuss successful entrepreneurs, we need to pause for a moment to define what success means. A personal vision is important, but profits are based on reality. Your vision may include owning a private Caribbean island, but if your business is a small luncheonette, it's not likely to get you there.

In a publicly traded company, there is an assumption that the business has or can assemble the resources to grow whenever the opportunity presents itself. That is not always the case in a privately held company. Therefore, the financial goals of your personal vision have to be grounded in the reality of your company's potential value.

Small business does not follow the rules of big business. An individual owner seldom has the resources to develop an entirely new product. Available capital limits the options for geographic expansion. Besides, once a company is stable and profitable, most owners are very reluctant to borrow a lot of money for expansion or new initiatives.

I am often asked, "How much *should* my company be making?" "Should" is a difficult term to define. In a small business, it is as much about non-financial factors as any dollar amount. There are no hard-and-fast rules for determining what any small business's margins should be, but there are some general benchmarks.

Profitability measures differ dramatically from business to business. A warehouse distribution company will never see the margins of a software developer. There are structural constraints in the wholesale industry that make such margins impossible.

Industries use varying benchmarks. Retailers might "keystone" their products with 100% markup over cost, or a 50% gross margin. All expenses come out of that margin. Manufacturers, on the other hand, typically put all the expenses of producing their products into cost of goods sold. COGS includes materials, direct labor, capital equipment, utilities, and any other expense related to the manufacturing process. Their margin after COGS covers only general and administrative expenses. It becomes difficult to ascertain with any accuracy whether a manufacturer's 30% margin is better or worse than a retailer's 50% margin.

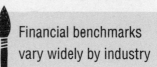

Financial benchmarks vary widely by industry

In professional service organizations, the metrics vary just as widely. Accounting firms frequently measure in terms of "profit before partner expenses." Those expenses include base salaries, health insurance, and continuing education, all of which are considered part of the profit. Law firms usually use the term "profit" to mean the surplus available for distribution to partners after those same expenses are paid.

Different industries even measure revenue differently. I know two business owners, one of whom has a large travel agency, and the other a large collection agency. Each company has about 120 employees, and each occupies a full floor of an office building.

The travel agency books about $140,000,000 annually in trips and fares. The collection agency receives about $140,000,000 in payments on behalf of its clients.

The travel agency earns about $5,000,000 in fees from its bookings. The collection agency keeps about $5,000,000 in fees from its collections.

The travel agency, according to the standard practices in its industry, is listed as a $140,000,000 company. The collection agency, also following the norms of its industry, describes itself as a $5,000,000 company.

I use these examples in coaching to show entrepreneurs how hearsay or anecdotal evidence can vastly over- or understate what you think another company or business is making. Often, an owner will come to me either excited or aghast at what another has described as his profitability. "I need to be in his business!" is a common reaction, or else it is, "I can't believe a company that big doesn't make any money!"

Unless you understand the normal metrics and terminology of a specific industry, you cannot reasonably compare profitability between companies. Even in the same industry, the measurements may be difficult to nail down. Before you put too much effort into calculating whether you are making an appropriate profit by comparing yourself to other companies, here is an example of what happened to a group of owners in the exact same business.

Charles Barrett, a successful automobile dealer specializing in high-end cars (Jaguar, Ferrari, and Maserati), once explained his attempt to compare profits with peers.

"We formed a group," he said, "standardized our accounting software, and committed to revamping every line item classification on our statements to a single standard. It was a huge effort, and in the end it was largely a waste of time."

I will spare you an extended quotation and just tell you what they discovered. Some dealers "floor planned" their inventory. That is when the dealer has a line of credit with a lender to pay the manufacturer for his inventory of unsold cars. It can represent millions of dollars, and those who finance inventory that way have substantially different interest expense than those who do not.

Some dealers own their real estate inside the dealership entity. Others own it personally and lease it to their companies, while still others lease from a third party.

Some dealers use the manufacturer's consumer credit arm financing for new cars. Some receive commissions for referring customers to a local lender. Some carry their own paper as a profit center in the dealership, while a few have their own finance companies as separate entities.

Even in purportedly identical businesses, an apples-to-apples comparison of profitability proved to be impossible. Using numbers from within your industry is better than trying to compare your company to completely different businesses, but even then, it has limitations.

Profitability Rules of Thumb

Because so many owners have asked, "How much *should* my company be making?" I have developed a few rules of thumb. These are completely unscientific, and are based solely on my personal observations. In addition, I have to caution you that they are subject to the wide vagaries of revenue and profit measurement within a given industry.

I define profit for this purpose as *operating profit* or *earnings before interest and taxes* (EBIT). Those in capital-intensive or financed-based industries may not find these as useful as most others will.

Profits
First, any business must pay its owner(s) salaries that are comparable to market rates for their work. If you are managing eight people in a $1,000,000 company and that is your entire responsibility, then you should probably be paying yourself $75,000 or so as a manager. If you are the primary salesperson in addition to being the manager, add on the amount you would be paying for that position as well.

After paying all employees, *including the owner*, appropriately for their work, a decently run small business should be keeping something close to 10% of its revenue as EBIT. The best-run small businesses can generate about 20% EBIT, but that isn't feasible in all industries.

If your business generates more than 25% operating profit, then you are likely enjoying one of a few scenarios. Either you: a) are manufacturing or producing a standardized offering and have reached a level where you have true economies of scale, b) have a proprietary product that is unique in its market, or c) are enjoying a market anomaly that creates a temporary shortage of your products or services.

Revenue per Employee
Knowledge companies comprise a substantial portion of entrepreneurial businesses in the United States. Their profitability can be difficult to measure because their biggest expense is talent. That talent is often compensated according to the revenue produced, whether or not the producer is an owner.

Professional and B2B services dominate knowledge industries. They include architecture and design, engineering, IT support, law, accounting, consulting, real estate sales and management, software development, web design, insurance, staffing, wealth management and most health care.

In professional services and other knowledge-based businesses, across many fields and industries, I have found a yardstick that holds up to general application.

- Companies producing less than $100,000 in revenue per employee (including both producers and support staff) are usually struggling, and in danger of failing.

- Between $100,000 and $150,000 per employee is usually sufficient to pay for talent and keep some profit for the owner.

- Between $150,000 and $200,000 per employee is enough to generate substantial ongoing profits and the working capital for growth.

- Companies that generate in excess of $200,000 per employee are highly successful, and often are leaders in their markets.

I am sure a number of readers might find themselves below one of these ranges and feel they are very successful, or perhaps exceed the ranges and think that they should be much more profitable. It really depends on your personal definition of success, but these are reasonable guidelines.

Seller's Discretionary Earnings

Seller's Discretionary Earnings or SDE is a measure used by business brokers to determine the "true" value of a company. It is something of a euphemism for "Benefits the company pays on behalf of the owner that would *really* be personal expenses if he was working for someone else."

Items included in SDE are limited only by the creativity of an individual owner, his or her tolerance for the risk of an IRS audit, and the cooperativeness of 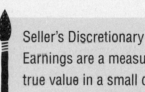 the company's accounting firm. I have seen some very aggressive approaches (like $300 a week at the grocery store to fund non-existent "employee appreciation events" for a company with a staff of five people) but here is a short list of common expenses that are normally considered SDE:

- retirement contributions to an owner's account
- non-qualified deferred compensation plans
- automobiles that aren't necessary for daily operations (not, for instance, a delivery truck that the owner just drives home at night)
- key man insurance payable to the owner's family
- travel and entertainment for family as board members or managers
- rent in excess of market rates for a building owned personally and rented to the company

- salary and benefits for family members not strictly
  necessary to run the business

- a second home occasionally lent to employees as an
  incentive

- professional fees (legal and accounting) for the
  owner's personal needs

- cellular phones and home broadband service also
  used by family

- dues, subscriptions and education not strictly related
  to the business

- charitable contributions by the company

All of these seller's discretionary expenses are part of the value
and benefit of owning a business, and should properly be included
when you are trying to calculate your profitability.

These measures of income and profit are useful for getting a rough
estimate of your company's success in comparison to others, but there
is no "standard." I've known owners who felt an income of $100,000
a year was impressive and others who regarded $20,000,000 as a "nice
start." Success is what you want it to be.

What is "Rich?"

Just as there is no universal measure of appropriate profitability, there
is no standard definition of "rich." It is probably the most personal
and subjective of measurements.

An owner once told me, "I worked in my business for over ten
years with the goal of making over $100,000 a year. Once I reached it,
it didn't seem like very much at all."

Almost any amount of money is a lot if you have none. To an
employee making $10 an hour, $50,000 a year is rich. To the owner
of a business collecting $100,000 a month in revenues, $50,000 at the
end of the year might seem poor compensation for all that work. It is
a matter of perspective.

A few years ago, my family spent our winter holidays skiing at Deer
Valley, Utah. If you've never visited, Deer Valley is undeniably a place

where wealthy folks gather. At the top of some lifts, there are homes that almost defy description. Some easily measure between 15,000 and 20,000 square feet overall, with amenities like a whole story encased in glass to highlight the indoor swimming pool.

My sons were young teenagers and were suitably impressed. On one ride up the chairlift, my youngest turned to me and asked "Dad, what is rich? My friends come to our house and say that we are rich, but you are always telling me that there are things we can't afford to buy. I know that we can't live in a house like one of these. How much money do you need to be rich?"

It was a great question, and I asked him to wait until dinner that night to discuss it. We went back to our condo (ten miles from the slopes—nice but not as convenient as I might have liked) and after preparing dinner, I returned to his question.

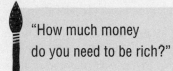

"How much money do you need to be rich?"

I told him that I thought there were four kinds of "rich."

Well-off: You are well-off when your work produces enough income to allow you the lifestyle you seek. You are able to afford a nice home and vacations to faraway places. You can sustain minor calamities, like a car repair or a broken water heater, by simply writing a check. You can eat in a restaurant whenever you chose, and not be concerned about how much the bill will be. I explained that to most people, that would define "rich."

Wealthy: Wealthy people have a lifestyle at least as nice as the well-off, but they also produce enough income to accumulate earning assets, things that will increase their income without requiring ongoing effort like stocks or rental property. Those assets help to build their net worth, but these people still have to continue working as their primary income-generating activity.

Rich: Rich people enjoy the lifestyle of their choice, but it is based on income from assets, not their personal labor. If they work, it's by choice; not for the income associated with their efforts.

Escape Velocity: Those who have reached escape velocity (a term I think was coined by Microsoft's Bill Gates) have sufficient income-producing assets that they can make any lifestyle choices, have no need to work, and at the end of each day, regardless of how much they spend, they go to bed with more money than they woke up with. A few people achieve escape velocity in their lifetimes, but many others were born at that level.

In answer to my son's question about our family, I told him we were well-off, were working on being wealthy, had aspirations of someday being rich, and had absolutely no shot at escape velocity. And by the way, escape velocity would probably be the required level to buy that swimming pool house he had his eye on.

A Bias for Implementation

One of the characteristics that define entrepreneurs, and the one they most frequently complain is lacking in their employees, is a sense of urgency. Hunters want to get things done. They have an abiding abhorrence of languishing projects. Stalled initiatives are rapidly relegated to the dustbin of forgotten history.

In working with hundreds of entrepreneurs, I've often had the opportunity to observe different companies in the same industry. Their products or services are essentially identical. They compete in the same market, and economic conditions they work in are consistent. Their strategic differentiation is minimal, if they enjoy any real differentiation at all.

> Most small businesses have minimal, if any, true strategic differentiation

Many of these businesses top out at a level where they provide the owner with a comfortable living, but require his constant attention to maintain. Frequently, that level is at about $1,000,000 in revenue. A million dollars of revenue seems to be a number that, for whatever reason, is both achievable and sustainable by most competent small business owners.

If we use the rule of thumb measures outlined previously, at a million dollars of revenue, an owner with eight employees should be earning around $200,000 a year in combined salary and profits. That would come with a reasonable $75,000 salary for management duties and a 12% operating margin.

Now, apply those same metrics to a similar business generating $5,000,000 a year in revenues. If the owner is drawing a salary three times larger for managing thirty-five employees ($225,000) and maintaining an operating profit of around 12%, he or she would be generating in the vicinity of $825,000 a year in personal income.

 A bias for implementation is a quiet urgency

Most people would classify a $200,000 annual income as well off. An $825,000 income would make someone wealthy, and probably well on the way to becoming rich. What is the difference between an entrepreneur whose company settles in at a million-dollar revenue level, and one who grows to $5,000,000?

Implementation.

A bias for implementation is a quiet urgency. It isn't running around shoving people forward. In fact, it really doesn't involve motivating others nearly as much as it requires disciplining yourself. It is the ingrained belief that once you decide to do something, nothing will stop you from doing it as quickly as possible.

Let me repeat this for emphasis. In the same industry, with similar markets and capabilities, the difference between an entrepreneur who makes $200,000 a year and one who makes $825,000 a year is the personal ability to implement.

My friend David Halpern, a lifelong business guru says, "The problem with most small business owners is they have a God-given right to procrastinate." They choose their own priorities, and can change them without asking anyone's permission.

An employee comes to you and asks "Boss, did you do that really important thing you said you would have done by today?" You respond, "No, because I had something more important to do instead." What does the employee say? Probably something like, "Okey dokey. Let me know when you get it done, please."

The late Stephen R. Covey, in his bestselling book *The Seven Habits of Highly Effective People*, divided tasks into four categories. Some are urgent and important. Some are important but not urgent. Some are urgent but not important and the rest are neither important nor urgent.

Many entrepreneurs can reach a modest level of success through their exceptional ability to juggle the things that are both important and urgent. They develop a reputation for dependability by delivering projects on deadline. They handle minor crises as they arise, while those around them are still analyzing the cause or placing blame. They maintain a decent level of profitability by watching expenses closely, and by acting quickly when costs get out of line.

Unfortunately, their constant focus on the urgent allows them to put off many things that are really important. New projects are sidelined until there is "enough time." Marketing materials, websites, or catalogs grow stale. Operating procedures evolve until their written documentation is so out of date that it is ignored by employees. Profit margins shrink because they don't analyze costs and pricing until it becomes a critical issue.

Highly successful entrepreneurs get to the next level by implementing the things that may not be urgent, but are vital to their company's growth. Covey's book offers some techniques for identifying what is really important and accomplishing it. There are dozens of other effective methodologies for getting on track. However, none of them works unless you develop a bias for implementation, and tackle new initiatives as part of your normal working day.

My favorite quote is from Albert Einstein, "Insanity is doing the same thing day after day and expecting a different result."

An entrepreneur's definition of success may be subjective, but the ability to reach it isn't. Successful hunters hunt. They decide what needs doing and they do it.

Chapter 13
Lifestyle vs. Legacy

BUSINESS OWNERS MAY THROTTLE BACK their personal effort when they achieve the *well-off* or the *wealthy* level of success. They don't lack ambition; they merely shift their focus to different priorities. They run their businesses to satisfy chosen lifestyles.

Other entrepreneurs continue to hunt long after they have achieved a level of success that easily exceeds my definition of *rich*. They've built a net worth that allows them to maintain their standard of living without working, but they continue to pour effort into their businesses.

Lifestyle Businesses

Most entrepreneurs have a personal vision that involves lifestyle. They work toward building a business that is sufficiently successful to finance a specific level of comfort for themselves and their families.

The range of lifestyle businesses is very broad. At one end are very small businesses with no employees. The entrepreneurs who run them define their preferred lifestyle as working from home, or working for only a few hours each day. Perhaps they don't want to deal with employees, or only seek supplementary income. Sometimes they build a business around their hobby or a personal interest. While these are often termed "lifestyle businesses" in the media, they are really jobs that provide someone with income without answering to a boss.

Throughout this book we talk about "companies," which are defined as a business that combines the efforts of a group of people to generate revenue. Most companies have a hunter/owner who employs at least a few farmers in the delivery of products or services.

A personal vision defines your parameters for success

An entrepreneur who builds a substantial company may still own a lifestyle business, depending on his or her personal vision. He may seek a nice retirement fund or the money to build a community outreach center. His ambition may be limited to paying for the children's'college education or as ambitious as traveling the world for half of each year. Any of these ambitions could be satisfied by a lifestyle business.

I know one successful entrepreneur who defines his personal vision as, "Selling this company for enough money to provide generational wealth, so that none of my descendants will ever have to worry about what they will do for a living."

As ambitious a goal as that may be, it is still within the definition of a lifestyle business. He is envisioning a business that tracks his working career. When the time comes, his lifestyle goals fund simultaneously with his departure from the business.

As we discussed earlier, entrepreneurs have a deep and personal attachment to their businesses. Most regard their companies as vehicles to achieve their personal objectives.

If an owner doesn't clearly set out a written personal vision, he still defines the parameters of success without realizing it. As the company begins to generate a comfortable lifestyle, he may start to slow down. Risks look riskier, and profits are more quickly taken out of the company. The good things in life, a second home, expensive automobile or travel to exotic locales, become achievable and are enjoyed more often.

Of course, the business must be stable enough to sustain a lifestyle while the owner is enjoying it. Some entrepreneurs fall into a roller coaster of good times alternating with bad times. They enjoy the fruits of their labor, right up until the wheels start coming off at the company and they have to plunge back into operations.

If you find yourself spending more time thinking about the benefits your business provides than you do about the business itself, step back. Write down your personal vision with goals for retirement age, financial security, assets, and the activities you want to enjoy, and determine how close you are to reaching them. If you are there, or near enough to see your goal, it may be time to start transferring your responsibilities to an SIC or SIT.

I know many owners who are stuck in a rut because of their self-image as a hard-charging go-getter. Although they are actually satisfied with where they are financially, they continually berate themselves for not doing more. Be honest with yourself.

Every so often, an entrepreneur builds a company that far exceeds his vision of success. There is a word for that: luck. The first century Roman philosopher **You are free to decide that you are successful enough** Seneca said, "Luck is when preparation meets opportunity." If you do things well, and conditions outside your control are favorable, you might just get lucky and exceed your own expectations.

Every entrepreneur defines his lifestyle goals differently. One of the wonderful things about owning a business is that you set your own limits. Usually that means choosing to be more successful than you are at present; but sometimes that means deciding that you are successful enough.

Most small businesses are entrepreneurial enterprises, vehicles to accomplish the owner's personal objectives. There is nothing wrong with that. Current social commentary may brand such thinking as selfish and self-centered. Other people emphasize your obligation to generate a better living for your employees, or assume that you carry an inherent obligation to create more jobs. My answer to that is succinct. Bullshit.

The hunters of 7,000 years ago did not suffer the discomfort and deprivation of the hunt because they felt some noble obligation to benefit the community at large. They hunted because, primarily, *they* wanted to eat. You take the risks of hunting for your own reasons. Do it for the lifestyle you desire, and treat those who help you fairly. That is the extent of your obligation.

Legacy Businesses

Some entrepreneurs don't slow down when they achieve their personal vision. They accelerate. They build enterprises that far exceed anything they need or want for themselves. They are the legacy builders.

I've worked with scores of company founders who achieved what any normal person considers exceptional success. For discussion purposes, let's peg that at a million dollars of personal income, year in and year out. Some make considerably more than that.

Most live modest lifestyles. There is no question of whether they have enough to fund their objectives. They have plenty for that, and yet they keep working to grow their businesses.

It's easy to brand such owners as greedy, but it simply isn't true. To paraphrase Bill Gates again, "Money is the best way we have of keeping score." For those entrepreneurs who are chasing accumulated wealth, it's not about what they might buy that they can't have today. It's about competition and keeping score. It is the same drive that sends hunters after the biggest trophy buck. That isn't building a legacy.

That doesn't include high technology billionaires. They clearly fall into the category of luck. When Mark Zuckerberg was sitting in his dormitory room programming the first version of Facebook, he wasn't saying, "Hey, I bet this will help me meet girls *and* make enough money to buy a medium-sized country!"

As an abstract scorecard, however, money isn't much of a motivator. A normal person experiences limited satisfaction from checking the bank balance every day. Most legacy business owners are normal people. They live in nice neighborhoods and drive nice cars, but they have no desire to own an island or a sports team. What drives them to keep growing a business far beyond their own financial needs?

Usually legacy builders set out to build lifestyle businesses. Many used their innate hunting talent and a bias for implementation to grow their business faster than they thought possible. A substantial number were relatively young when the lifestyle capabilities of their companies reached their goal, and they simply were not ready to walk away. Some did not get there until much later in life.

In both cases, the legacy builders reached their personal goals, and realized that they had the ability and resources to set another goal, one much larger than their lifestyle objectives. They began to think of their companies as vehicles for bigger things than their own comfort.

George Rapier, MD founded WellMed, a primary care group focused on senior care. The business grew rapidly, and within its first decade had grown to multiple offices in Texas, along with similar ventures in Florida and Indiana.

As a practicing physician, Dr. Rapier made a comfortable income, although as a CEO he experienced both highs (an equity stake purchased by an investment fund) and lows (a layoff of over 20% of the employees). Eventually WellMed stabilized, and currently has twenty-four offices.

As the business grew and became more profitable, George regularly received inquiries from prospective purchasers. Any of these offers would have been sufficient to allow him to live in **Some entrepreneurs discover a vision bigger than their personal lifestyle** luxury for a lifetime. He knew that the company had outgrown his executive abilities, and seriously wanted to surrender his role as an active CEO. Even more, he wanted WellMed to be a continued source of benefit to the community, and worried that it might not happen under someone else's ownership.

Eventually, George developed a plan that satisfied his legacy objectives. In 2011, he sold a controlling interest of the management company to a large health care organization, while maintaining control of the core physician group. With the proceeds from that sale, he started a charitable foundation that has become a major force in the South Texas community. It funds research, education, and medical facilities for both seniors and the underprivileged. George's business became a legacy that will live on long after he has fully retired.

Legacy entrepreneurs have moved beyond personal gain. Some use their hunting talents to benefit scores, and often hundreds of employees, but that doesn't satisfy them. They use their abilities in the service of broader objectives. Their vision shifts to building something that has nothing to do with personal lifestyle, but instead aims to change at least a part of the world.

Most of the legacy hunters I know didn't start out that way. In the beginning, they were trying to create a lifestyle business like most other entrepreneurs. Along the way, they experienced success that could permit them to engender real change. Entrepreneurs like these are the driving force behind much of what is great about capitalism.

Whether your ambition is to build a lifestyle or a legacy, you bring others along with you. Some entrepreneurs create livelihoods for employees. Others build legacies that extend beyond their lifetimes. Either way, the 3% of the population who take the risks and build new things create opportunities for the millions of farmers who follow.

Chapter 14
Going the Distance

IF YOU ARE A BUSINESS OWNER, I have some good news and some bad news. The good news is that you are your own boss. The bad news is that you have a lousy boss. There is one huge downside to being an entrepreneur. You can't quit.

Johnny Paycheck's classic Country and Western song *Take this Job and Shove It* has become a standard for DJs at weddings and class reunions because it strikes a chord with everyone who has ever had a bad day at work. For the farmers of the world, it is the one thing over which they have ultimate control. If the job gets too tough, too demanding or too unreasonable, they can choose to move on.

Business owners have fewer options. They can't say, "That's not my job." Everything in the company is ultimately their job. If your biggest customer makes unreasonable demands, you can meet them or risk losing a critical revenue source. If an employee's performance is unacceptable, you choose between having a job done poorly and not having it done at all. If you have a busy season, it probably governs when you can plan vacations or family activities.

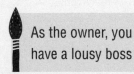

As the owner, you have a lousy boss

The mantle of ownership rests lighter on some days, but there aren't many days when you can just decide not to make decisions, or not to solve problems. It comes with the territory. You wanted control and, like it or not, you have it.

A Job vs. a Business

If owning your company is a lousy job, the uncomfortable reality is you *made* it that way. It sounds cold, but it is true. As an owner, you decide what your company does, what its culture is, and how you will deliver your product or service. You built this house, and now you have to live in it.

Earlier, we discussed why many hunters, especially those who began as Technicians, feel an obligation to produce more than any employee. It is their justification for making more money than anyone else in the company. Successful entrepreneurs get past that perceptual handicap, and understand that their role is far more important than just producing the product.

If you own a business, you can lead employees by example, direction, or command, but you lead them. It is not a choice. Sometimes your leadership is the only thing that stands between the company and imminent disaster.

Christine Prescott owns Corporate Travel Planners (CTP). She is a Technician, who started out as a travel agent and worked her way up to owning a major agency. In the travel industry, to say that 2001 was a difficult year would be a dramatic understatement.

Airlines had reduced agent commissions several times in preceding years, but on September 1, 2001, they eliminated them entirely. Travel agents worldwide were still reeling from the loss of revenue when, on September 11th, terrorists hijacked four jumbo jets and flew them into the World Trade Center, The Pentagon, and a field in Pennsylvania. In an unprecedented move, the Federal Aviation Authority grounded virtually all non-military US air traffic for the next three days, stranding hundreds of thousands of travelers.

> A leader's job is to determine the objective, teach people how to reach it, and motivate them to do so

Thousands of those travelers were Christy's clients. They were stuck all over the world, making frantic calls to CTP for cars or hotel rooms. Every one of them wanted to reserve a seat on the first available flight after the skies reopened. CTP kept over 100 agents on the phones trying to help their customers.

Large travel agents enable automatic transfers between their bank accounts and those of the airlines. As flights were cancelled and tickets refunded, the carriers reached into CTP's bank accounts to reclaim hundreds of thousands of dollars in commissions paid before September 1st. The replacement reservations carried zero commission, so there was no opportunity to replace the lost revenue.

Christy was paying employees who couldn't generate income, while the carriers were draining away her cash reserves. Add to that her staff's shock and dismay about the attacks, and Corporate Travel Planners was on very shaky ground indeed.

Through all of it, Christy kept bouncing through the office like a cheerleader. She told her staff that everything was going to be fine, and kept them relaying the same message to her clients. "We are here, and we are going to help you."

Facing an unprecedented national disaster, disappearing reserves, and a bleak outlook for the future, Christy maintained her calm throughout. Months later, I asked her how she kept her act together. What she said will stay with me forever.

"I had no choice," she told me. "In every employee's eyes I saw fear. They thought we were finished. If I had shown a crack in my attitude, even for a moment, people would have been trampled in the rush for the door." Christy's tenacity, her refusal to even *consider* defeat, was the only thing that fended off oblivion for CTP.

Leadership is part of an owner's job. Sometimes you don't have a choice about accepting it, and doing it well, if you want your business to survive.

There are thousands of books and classes on leadership, and this is not one of them, except in the broadest sense. I have a simplified definition, which I think sums up everything you need to know.

A leader's job is to determine the objective, teach people how to reach it, and motivate them to do so.

The difference between a having job and owning a business is your leadership.

Time to Lead

Every minute you spend working *in* your business is one subtracted from working *on* your business. Every iota of personal production reduces the time you spend leading; and time is inflexible.

My friend Nicholas Economou has taught time management for years. He begins each new seminar with an observation. We each have twenty-four hours in a day, and each hour has sixty minutes containing sixty seconds. There just isn't any more time. We all get the same.

> No definition of leadership includes doing more work than anyone else

You can't make time. You can't save time. You can't stretch, steal, compress or shift time. Every second that passes is the past. There is no time reclamation.

Nicholas teaches that the terms we use for time are really terms for commitment. If you say, "I don't have the time," you are actually saying, "I have different priorities I choose instead." If you say, "I ran out of time," you are really saying that you didn't plan well enough, or that you let something more urgent take the place of the deadline.

Covey's division of responsibilities—important and urgent—requires choosing where to spend your time. In making the commitment to lead, it means choosing to spend time leading—not doing.

Time is the standard excuse of owners who aren't leading. If you constantly tell your employees that you are "too busy," don't be surprised when monthly financial statements are late or orders don't ship because, "We didn't have the time."

Just as you cannot avoid the burdens of ownership, you can't sidestep the role of leadership. If the message you are sending to your employees is that doing the work is the most important thing in the business; they will focus on *doing* the work. Whether doing their work generates the results you seek is an entirely different issue.

Returning to Doug Tatum's wisdom, *No Man's Land* is where an owner does the work of three people for the pay of three people. Time is inflexible. No matter how bright or proficient you are, you *really* can't do the work of three people, or at least not do it well. Doing it correctly would require three people.

"That's easy for you to say" is a normal response. No one plans to take on the work of three people. They usually do it because they think there isn't enough *money* to hire more employees. That simply isn't true. Employees should be hired to *add* profit, not reduce it.

Successful entrepreneurs use a simple formula to determine whether they can afford an additional hire. If the work the new employee will do frees someone else to do work that generates more profit, it is a necessary hire. If the work they will do frees up *your* time, then you need to use that time to generate more than it costs to pay the employee.

Which is more profitable, filling an order or calling on a new customer? Closing a sale or answering a request for proposal? Estimating a job or training a supervisor to bring the current job in under budget?

In most scenarios, you can use your time to do things that are more important and more profitable than the job you are filling now. The things you would Leadership is choosing where to spend your time do with more time are usually the things that made your business successful in the first place (and are likely the things you enjoy).

You might cover a need using less expensive methods than full-time employment. With today's technology, a new position might be part-time, shared, telecommuted, virtual, or contracted. Whatever your budget, it need only be enough to allow you to do more with *your* time.

Hiring the Best

A business owner can't quit, can't burn out, and can't abdicate the decision making process. How can you maintain the level of attention and commitment needed to grow a business over long periods?

Successful business owners have a deceptively simple answer. Hire the best. Not the best people you can afford or the best people available. Hire the *best*. Whether a position calls for a hunter or a farmer, get a great one.

I have a client who sets the same goal for himself every single month. He has 100 employees, and the business is growing rapidly, yet his primary objective is always identical. "This month," he will say, "I need to hire one or two more really great people."

Small business owners hire too quickly and fire too slowly. They settle for good enough. If you have an administrative assistant, she should answer the phone correctly every time. She should remember who the important customers are, and form relationships with them. If she handles correspondence, her output should be letter perfect and ready for sending when she presents it to you for signature. You don't have the time to waste being a proofreader.

Hunters are leaders, not managers. Leading communicates an expectation of competence. If you are acting as the last check on employees' work, you are failing to lead. Your employees see that their work does not have to be flawless, merely good enough. They can depend on you to make it perfect.

There is a measure of ruthlessness that is required to build a great company, regardless of its size. The more focused you become on surrounding yourself with people who can be great, the less of your own energy is needed to manage. That saved energy is what you use to grow a successful business.

It is lonely at the top. Carrying the burden of success for an entire organization is tough enough on any given day, and for a business owner it is a marathon without a finish line. To make it, you have to be able to share the load. The stark reality is that you are the only one who can hire and train those with whom you will share it.

If a great business depends on excellent employees, how can you attract and retain them against the resources of larger corporations? Getting the best means hiring employees who are very good at what they do, and who are getting better all the time. Of course, your competition will be companies with greater resources than yours, vying for the same people.

Salary and benefits are important, and it is often difficult for a small business to match the employment packages of a big corporation. An entrepreneur has to make a leap of faith. Should you spend the money for people who will make you more successful, or do you wait to be more successful before you spend the money on getting the best people?

I admit that it's a Catch-22, but you can't improve your quality of life surrounded by mediocre performers.

Small businesses present an attractiveemployment alternative to big organizations for a litany of reasons.

An employee in a small business is an individual. Others in the company know who he, and his role is in the organization. He does not have to search the cafeteria at lunchtime to find someone to eat with. He doesn't have a job description defined by a Roman numeral (Level IV *anything*) or shared with a dozen others.

People want to be important. Big businesses can tell people they are important, but reality intrudes when It is lonely at the top they are sitting in a cube farm that stretches over the horizon. In a small business, every employee really *is* a key part of the machine. It is an owner's job to make sure that is understood, both by each employee and by every one of his or her coworkers.

Everyone wants to make a difference. Imagine standing outside of the exit gate from a large corporation's employee parking lot. Pretend that each employee rolls down the car window and answers two questions: "Did you do a good job today?" and "How do you know?"

Most will answer "Yes" to the first question and "I don't know" to the second.

Enthusiasm for a job has to come from more than slogans and team meetings. It should be generated by an understanding of *why* a job is important, and how it affects the whole company. A small

Hire slowly, fire quickly, and invest in the best business owner enjoys a tremendous advantage when communicating that information to every employee. Simply because of your proximity, you have a greater opportunity to tell each employee why he is an important part of what your company does.

Knowing that they are doing important work, that they are an important part of the business, and that there exists an opportunity to become even *more* important, is what great employees seek in their jobs.

Great employees make you money. Poor employees cost you money. Hire slowly, fire quickly, and invest in the best. It is the most effective use of your money possible.

Chapter 15
Rocks in the Road

SOMETIMES THE BURDEN of responsibility weighs heavily on a business owner. Everyone has days when they fantasize about doing something else. That is why recharging time is so important for an entrepreneur's mental health. Vacations are not merely a reward; they are necessary to maintain your mental conditioning.

Carrying too much on your shoulders can have an adverse effect. Over a long period, the impact can be psychological, physiological, or both. We call the psychological symptoms *Burnout,* and the physical ones *Adrenalin Deficit.*

Burnout

One of the most important questions I ask of an owner who wants to sell his business is, "Why do you want to sell?" If his answer is, "I'm just burned out," I know what I will likely find.

Sales probably stalled several years before. If the revenues have not declined, then profits have. The business is likely dependent on a limited group of long-term customers or on one big low-margin account.

Employee turnover is high, or (just as bad) no one ever quits. If there is a sales department, they are primarily order-takers. If there is a purchasing function, they are merely submitting reorders as inventory is drawn down.

Most importantly, the owner has a job. He is indispensable to the daily functioning of the company. The business revolves around him.

To quote Kevin Armstrong of Vancouver again, "The more you work in your business, *the less it is worth*." I suggest that entrepreneurs have that phrase tattooed on their chests.

The more I work in my business, the less it is worth

When they look in the mirror each morning, it can be a reminder that their personal work has little to do with how successful their company is.

Burnout is cruel. It not only takes a toll on an owner, but on the rest of the company as well. Looking to the owner for leadership, employees find someone who is only going through the motions. They begin just going through the motions themselves.

Lacking positive leadership, employees often develop a culture of complaining, *especially* if the owner complains in front of them. Those who are seeking real career opportunities leave. Those who remain want to do as little as they can get away with.

The very conditions that made the owner hit the wall in the first place, too many duties, too many hours, and too much responsibility, already detract from the value of the business. No Acquirer wants to buy a lousy job. Many wind up with one, but very few will shell out good money to start out that way.

> Burnout is the loss of control

A burnt-out owner's role is untenable. He is running a business that isn't worth very much, and it is worth less every day that he continues to run it. By the time he realizes that he no longer has a successful business, it is often too late. I've seen scores of owners watch their lifetime's work, and their lifetime's investment, dissipate completely before they understood what was happening to them.

Burnout is the loss of control. You own a business because you wanted control over your destiny. Letting the business consume you is the furthest thing from control you can imagine. Working until you can't do any more has limited benefit and no potential. If your excuse is, "I can't help it. I have to do this," then you have forgotten how to be a hunter. You are enslaved by the crop cycle.

Burning out from the *job* of running a business is avoidable. It requires a vision, some planning, and a lot of commitment. It takes focused energy, and the willpower to not to drift into being a mere engine of effort. Investing the energy now is less difficult than the will it takes to work day after day once you're burned out. As a classic ad slogan says, you can pay now or you can pay later.

If you fear that burnout is creeping up on you, return to your personal vision. What do you expect to accomplish from owning your own business? Look at the time off from work required to do what you wish to do. Calculate the amount of income you'll need to implement your plans.

Pull out the organizational chart you drew earlier. If you skipped that exercise, try it now. It may be easier to build it from the bottom up.

How many first-line workers will it take to generate enough revenue to fulfill your personal vision? Determine how many production workers, warehousemen, drivers, or average-billing professionals would create the revenue needed. From there, it is fairly easy to work your way up the ladder.

How many supervisors or managers would be required to train and monitor those workers? How many executives for the managers? What **The more you work in your business, the less it is worth** specialties of yours could eventually become full-time jobs for someone else? If your vision requires over fifty people, you probably want to add some human resource and information technology support.

Once you have built your successful organization on paper, you can start filling in boxes. Avoid the temptation of putting current employees at the top of the pyramid. Unless they are exceptional hunters, most will not be able to keep pace with you for the whole journey. Place loyal employees in the position that matches their greatest probable potential.

Without drafting a business strategy or a budget, you have created a long-term plan and a defense against burnout. As your business grows, you can more easily see when it is appropriate to fill in another box with a name instead of a position description. You can think about what the most effective next hire will be. You can identify employees with potential and begin grooming them for future positions.

Most importantly, you can objectively identify when you *need more help*. Burnout comes when you take on as much as you can, more often than you should. Waiting until you are drowning leaves you unfit to hire and train the best people.

The corollary to, "The more you work in your business the *less* it is worth" isn't "The less you work in your business the *more* it is worth." It is, "The less *you* do of the work in the business, the more it is worth."

A successful entrepreneur is one whose business provides the material, social, and spiritual benefits he wants, *along with the time to enjoy them.* I've never met a business owner who achieved this level of success, and was also in danger of burning out.

That does not mean that the most successful of entrepreneurs don't face crises. The responsibilities of owning a business can become overwhelming without warning. Even the most successful entrepreneurs can sometimes be pushed to the wall.

The Other ADD

There is another kind of ADD. I call it *Adrenalin Deficit Disorder*. It is very real, and although it can affect others besides business owners, it hits entrepreneurs disproportionately often.

Adrenalin Deficit Disorder strikes when you can least afford it, robbing you of the physical ability to think and act quickly in a crisis. It can render an entrepreneur incapable of leading when it is most needed.

I began reading about the effects of adrenalin after going through a crisis early in my business career. Our adrenal gland is one of nature's miracles. Triggered as part of our instinctive "fight or flight" reaction in an emergency, it floods your bloodstream with a powerful stimulant. It allows you to go faster and harder … for a while. Of course, there is a price to pay.

Studies indicate about a one-to-one ratio between the time you overuse adrenalin and the time it takes to recover. There is also a correlation between the intensity of the adrenalin flow and the recovery time. Getting psyched up to play a touch football game may cost you a couple hours of fatigue (compounded by your physical effort) afterward. Spending five minutes saving a child from a burning building could well require the same multiple-hour recovery time.

> The less you do of the work, the more your business is worth

When a business has a problem, the owner frequently calls on adrenalin to cope with it. I'm sure that you've had a day when everything went badly. The problems were waiting for you when you walked in the door, and kept compounding. If you are like many owners, you cranked your normal intensity up a notch to deal with the chaos. Perhaps you moved faster, thought faster, and talked faster than anyone around you. You might have lost your temper and yelled at employees or vendors. At the end of the day, you were exhausted. It's likely you went home and collapsed in front of the TV or went to bed early.

That was adrenalin, the oldest companion of a hunter. Adrenalin allowed the hunter to run a little faster and jump a little higher at critical moments. It also helped him dodge a swiping claw or a stabbing antler. Any good hunter can call on adrenalin at will.

When a company is in a survival situation, when everything is on the line, an owner doesn't have the luxury of a recovery period. Days are long, problems are constant, and everyone is turning to you. That is when you call on your adrenalin to carry you through, not for minutes or days, but for weeks and months. It can work, but there is a price to pay. Eventually your body submits the bill.

Dennis Stahl owns Lone Star Pet Supply (LSPS), a large and very successful distributor of pet foods and supplies. His company sells almost 20,000 line items, from stainless steel dog bowls to aquariums, and from chew toys to special veterinary diets. Of course, they also sell dog food. They sell *a lot* of dog food.

Adrenalin is the oldest companion of the hunter

Through the 1990's LSPS grew its relationship with Iams, a manufacturer of premium pet foods. When Clay Mathile, the owner of Iams, made a strategic decision to limit the number of Iams distributors in the United States, he chose Lone Star as their exclusive distributor for most of Texas and Louisiana. In return, LSPS sold Iams exclusively to its pet store customers. Dennis ran a great company and was a fixture on the Iams Dealer Advisory Council, flying several times a year to discuss industry trends with the corporation's top executives.

Iams sold its products exclusively to independent pet stores, breeders and veterinarians. For the independent pet store owner, it was a major differentiation to offer a premium food that wasn't available in the local supermarket or chain store. Those small businesses saw Iams as their chief tool to attract regular repeat customers, and regarded the Lone Star salespeople as Iams' representatives to their pet stores.

In August of 1999, Clay Mathile made a surprise announcement. He had sold the company to Proctor and Gamble, the consumer products giant. The independent pet industry waited with bated breath to see what would happen.

It wasn't a very long wait. In spring of 2000, P&G began shipping Iams foods to its traditional customers, big grocery and discount chains all over the country. The pet store owners were enraged. For decades they had promoted Iams as being better than what any mass merchant had; now the mass merchants were selling "their" food at a discount.

Lone Star had spent years promoting its exclusive relationship to Iams, and successfully developed a reputation as the face of Iams in its territory. The independent dealers couldn't strike directly at Iams, but they could lash out at Lone Star, and lash out they did. Within 10 days of the first appearance of Iams in discount stores, Lone Star's revenues declined by 36%. Most of their core customers immediately began buying other brands from Lone Star's competitors. In all, the company's gross profit fell by 50% in two weeks.

Dennis had worked long days for months since the announcement, preparing for the inevitable firestorm of reaction. Nothing, however, could have prepared him for *this*. Lone Star's business model relied on high volumes of pet food to make it work. Without big bags of kibble, small shops couldn't reach the minimums for free truck delivery. Without free delivery, they wouldn't order the profitable leashes and chew toys that made up for Lone Star's low margins on pet food. Without a certain number of orders, Lone Star's long haul truck fleet couldn't cover its costs.

The most insidious thing about adrenalin deficit is that it steals your ability to react just when you need it the most. Buffeted by a flood of customer defections, Dennis began to withdraw from his staff, and found it difficult to make decisions. Finally, faced with both his own and the company's collapse, he did the only thing he could do; he broke his contract to sell Iams exclusively and signed on to distribute a competing brand. P&G threatened cancellation, but Dennis had proven to his customers that he was still on their side.

Slowly, the business began to come back. Customers realized that Lone Star had been hurt as badly as they were, and supported new lines as Dennis added them. The company finally resumed its growth curve, but Dennis frankly admits that it was nearly an entire year before he felt like himself again. It was the price he had to pay for living on adrenalin until he almost ran out.

The Old Testament story of David and Goliath supports our belief that the little guy always has a chance. However, as Mark Twain once said, "Let your sympathies and your compassion be always with the underdog in the fight—this is magnanimity; but bet on the other one—this is business."

This is a case where David won, eventually. In 2010, Lone Star Pet Supply gave notice to Proctor and Gamble Corporation that it was dropping their line of pet foods. The story of the local distributor who faced down a Fortune 50 giant made Dennis almost legendary in his industry.

The biggest problem with adrenalin deficit is the rebuilding time. If you hit the wall while the crisis is ongoing, you have no reserves available to deal with day-to-day problems. If you are fortunate enough or strong enough to last through the entire crisis, you won't have much left when the time comes for new initiatives.

Dennis Stahl's story is dramatic because it traces back to a single event, one day when everything changed. Thousands of business owners experienced similar drains on their emotional and physical reserves during the Great Recession. They faced the first signs of the downturn by ramping up their personal efforts. When that proved insufficient, they reduced staff, usually adding to their own responsibilities. As a slow year was followed by a miserable year, they reduced head count again, and took even more on themselves.

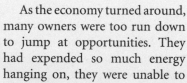

Exhausting your adrenalin leaves you unable to lead when it is most necessary

As the economy turned around, many owners were too run down to jump at opportunities. They had expended so much energy hanging on, they were unable to reach out for the next rung on the ladder. That may be one reason why a recovery, projected to be led by small business, was much slower than expected.

For most people, the end of a crisis is a legitimate cause to rest. Hunters or athletes who expend huge amounts of energy to reach a goal frequently go into near collapse once it is reached. If a salesman sells double his normal output in the week before a contest deadline, how likely is he to do it again in the first week that follows?

The danger of exhausting your adrenalin reserves is that you can't move quickly when an opportunity presents itself. Having survived a company-threatening event, you are more risk averse. Adding a new initiative to your workload seems impossible. You may avoid hiring, because you remember the pain of letting go employees who depended on you.

The hunter who hesitates loses the shot. One reason why a high percentage of successful companies start in a bad economy is they are founded by hunters who are willing to zig when others zag. They take risks when others are holding back. They have conserved their adrenalin for when it is most valuable.

A hunter's ability to rise to another level of performance is an asset. It should be a resource that is metered just like cash or employee hours. If you lean on it until it runs out, it won't be there when you need it the most.

Chapter 16
Success...Now What?

MOST BUSINESS OWNERS WORK HARD to be successful. Most books about entrepreneurs talk about success as an event in the future. For some business owners, the future is now. No discussion of the mind of an entrepreneur could be complete without talking about the end game. What happens when you succeed?

I've worked with many entrepreneurs who have become highly successful. They make a lot of money. (For measuring success in running a small business, I consider a personal income of more than $1,000,000 a year to be "a lot" of money.)

These owners have built companies that can thrive without them. Whether they are lifestyle or legacy owners doesn't matter. They have managers who execute the tasks of the business flawlessly, and who make necessary corrections to keep it on track. They come and go as they please. They take as many vacations as they wish, whenever and wherever they choose to go.

It sounds idyllic, but some of these owners aren't happy. They have lost their identity. They become unsure of their value, their personal contribution to the company's success. I've had dozens of conversations that started like this:

"I just came back from vacation. I told my managers to call me only if there was an emergency ... and nobody called. I returned to a few routine emails in my inbox. I dropped in on my key managers and asked them if there was anything they needed to discuss with me. They all said no. We set a sales record last month while I was away. I might as well not go in at all."

"I worked for years to get to this level. I know it is everything I dreamed of, but it doesn't feel like success. Something is missing. I'm not enjoying it nearly as much as I thought I would."

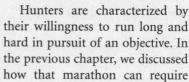

Financial success is not a guarantee of happiness

Hunters are characterized by their willingness to run long and hard in pursuit of an objective. In the previous chapter, we discussed how that marathon can require personal sacrifice, and sometimes brings with it psychological and physiological consequences. After you succeed, there are new challenges. There are psychological adjustments to make that not all entrepreneurs can easily handle.

As one successful owner told me, "I feel like the dog that caught the pickup truck. Now what?"

I label this phenomenon *reverse depression*. It is a nonsensical term, but I am reaching for a concept that is difficult to explain even for those experiencing it. They have achieved a work/life balance they previously only imagined. They have all the material trappings of success they desire. They are respected in the community. They have nailed both Maslow's hierarchy and their personal visions. They don't understand why it doesn't feel *better*.

Reverse depression is a feeling that things aren't the way they are supposed to be while all evidence points to the contrary. It is participating in the activities, or owning the material possessions you dreamed of, but being unable to take as much pleasure in them as you anticipated. It's crossing the finish line without experiencing the exhilaration that should come with winning the race.

Hunters must hunt. They aren't necessarily compulsive, but there is an inner drive that doesn't go away just because a goal is met. They need to be doing something productive. They are like Jessica Rabbit in *Who Framed Roger Rabbit*, who says, "I'm just drawn that way."

Hunting is setting a goal and focusing on execution. When hunters can't hunt, they frequently find some other trouble to get into. The same is true for entrepreneurs who have lost their sense of purpose.

Redefining an identity from struggling entrepreneur to successful business owner takes different paths with different people. In general, they fall into three categories: the Abdicators, the Prevaricators and the Progressives.

Abdicators

As you might infer from the label, Abdicators are the owners who walk away from their businesses. Often, abdication is really a form of burnout. Lacking a clear idea of what they should be doing, Abdicators stop doing *anything* to build the company. They leave the business in the hands of their managers and hope for the best.

Some Abdicators set out to have "fun." With too much time on their hands, they look for ways to spend their money. I've seen entrepreneurs who lose their sense of purpose become alcoholics, drug abusers, and compulsive gamblers.

Some become "investors," glorying in those worlds, like filmmaking or horseracing, where people with plenty of money to lose can surround themselves with glamorous sycophants.

Paradoxically, many get divorced. They discover that the spouse who stood behind them while they were building the company isn't nearly as interested as they are in a complete change of lifestyle.

Not all Abdicators travel the dark path of sin and depravity. Some throw themselves into ministry or community service. They travel on lengthy missions to the third world, or volunteer to staff Red Cross facilities after natural disasters. Those are laudable activities, but they are every bit as dangerous to the business if they remove you entirely.

Unless the Abdicator is fortunate enough to have an exceptional hunter as SIC, the business will likely continue to perform tomorrow much as it did yesterday. Eventually the competitive

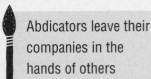

Abdicators leave their companies in the hands of others

climate will change. There is new technology, customers shift to a replacement product, or a key employee quits.

The key difference between the owner of any company and a top manager isn't brains, the ability to make decisions, or even vision. It is the owner's ability to make choices that involve risk. When the owner abdicates, those running the company are deprived of the ability to take risks. Their driving force shifts from growing the business to preserving the owner's income.

Eventually, most Abdicators are unwillingly drawn back into their businesses. The company's performance (and so their personal income) starts to decline, or there is a crisis that none of the employees are capable of addressing. When owners are *forced* to return, they often face an overwhelming array of issues. They may be unprepared to deal with new adversity, and may face a company culture that is much different from the one they left.

Abdication is a seductive scenario. Although an entrepreneur has devoted his or her life to a business, it can be tempting to start treating it like any other investment. The Abdicator starts regarding the company as one big 401K and abdication as the equivalent of retirement.

Entrepreneurial organizations aren't investments. They are living, breathing organisms that require leadership and the ability to adapt to change. If you are tempted to abdicate, do yourself and your employees a big favor. Sell the company to someone who will lead it, and use the proceeds for a more appropriate (and less risky) investment.

Prevaricators

Prevaricators don't leave their companies, but they don't exactly stay either. They use the freedom created by their success to do what they want, and do it only when they choose. Their lack of consistency creates all kinds of other problems. This is by far the most common reaction to the loss of purpose that characterizes reverse depression.

Prevaricators are in and out, off and on, here and there. Unfettered by rules or by anyone with the authority to tell them "no," they seek purpose on a serial basis, often to the dismay of those who work for them. There are a thousand ways that the Prevaricator can insert himself into new roles. Here are some of the most common:

The Super Technician

The Super Technician is an owner who most obviously suffers from too much time on his hands. Unsure of how to fill a day that doesn't present a plate-full of crises; he helps the business by doing what he "does best." He buries himself in a project until it becomes boring and leaves it for someone else to finish. He closes a big new account, but makes service commitments that are forbidden to the salespeople. He tinkers with processes on the most basic levels, ignoring the fact that he has managers who are responsible for those areas. He jumps into and out of tasks as the resident technical genius, without teaching others what he knows.

The Seagull

A seagull manager flies into the room, takes a crap on your desk, and flies away. This Prevaricator does the same thing, but involves the whole company. He comes into the office occasionally. Sometimes he is scheduled for a few days a week; sometimes it is completely at random. When he arrives, however, he expects the full attention of everyone. He demands reports and meetings, and sucks resources from day-to-day operations.

The Fixer

The Fixer "improves" the business using "Management by Walking Around." He perceives himself as the wellspring of all critical knowledge, the roving compendium of process and procedure. He dispenses unrequested advice and makes undocumented policy changes. Typically, he skips levels of supervision to get "right to the problem" and leaves confused employees in his wake.

The Dealmaker

This owner focuses his energies on business development. Confident that he has a management team that can handle anything; he proudly finds things to push them to new heights. Frequently, these take the form of "strategic alliances" with other business owners that draw the company into new areas, or which require development

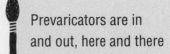

Prevaricators are in and out, here and there

of new capabilities. He doesn't worry about the challenges of implementation, but rather regards every initiative successfully handled by his employees to be justification for starting another.

The Split Personality

This is the most dangerous of all the Prevaricators. This owner typically announces that building a successful business has taught him the skills needed to build *any* business. He discounts the difficulty of the learning curve in his own industry, and regards other businesses as simpler than the one he built. Here are a few examples that I've worked with:

- The owner of a chain of mental health clinics who opened a restaurant

- The owner of an auto parts distributor who opened a chain of retail sporting goods stores

- The owner of a construction company who purchased an engine fuel conversion franchise

- The owner of a manufacturing company who opened a bar

- The owner of a software development company who started a telecommunications business

- The owner of a restaurant chain who started a nightclub

- The owner of an engraving company who purchased a dating service

- The owner of a manufacturing company who opened a surgery center

All of these entrepreneurs had built businesses successful enough to allow them ample free time. All said the same things when they bought or started their new ventures. "I understand the numbers. I have a good team of people who will help me. I have a partner (or employee, *or relative*) who knows about this new business. I'm too experienced to get in over my head."

Every one of these new ventures failed, at least in their original form. Most of these undertakings slowed down the growth of the original enterprise. A few were crippling, and two took everything else (including the owner's core business) down with them. In fact, after more than thirty years in business, I'm still waiting to see the founder of a business become successful by splitting his or her attention between it and another, unrelated venture. The results are never good.

"If you chase two rabbits, both will escape."
—Chinese proverb

Prevaricators aren't deadly to a business just because of what they do. They are damaging because of *how* they do it. Some of them come and go. Some try to function at both the top and the bottom of the organization. Others distract the employees by demanding attention for their *whim du jour*. It is their inconsistency that is so detrimental. Every company requires a steady hand at the wheel. If it isn't going to be yours, then let it be someone else's.

Progressives

Progressives, as the name implies, are those who move on. They don't fall prey to an identity crisis. They find a new purpose, that of growing to a higher level of leadership.

Nancy Kudla founded dNovus RDI in a spare bedroom of her home. She was my client for eight years, and is still a good friend. I won't steal her thunder (she is writing her own book) by telling you about the many challenges and successes that made up her journey. I will just stick to some basic background.

Nancy was a cadet in the first female class admitted to the US Air Force Academy. In her sophomore year she developed an astigmatism, which at that time put an end to her dream of being America's first female jet fighter pilot. Graduating with honors in both economics and international affairs, Nancy served for five years in the Air Force and, was honorably discharged as a captain.

Like most entrepreneurs, Nancy started her company as a Technician. Although she had many skills, she was amazingly adept at dissecting a government request for proposal (RFP), and writing a winning response.

There is an old saying in consulting. To be successful, you must sell the client what he wants, deliver what he needs, and get paid for it. Nancy could wade through an RFP and write a response that stood out because it not only addressed what the client wanted, but it told him what he really needed while still fitting it into the scope of the original request.

Her company grew from the guest bedroom to offices that housed twenty employees, then forty and eventually into its own building that held over sixty people. Satellite offices added more, and on-site employees at customer locations brought more still. dNovus RDI eventually employed over 300 people in multiple sites nationwide.

Along the way, Nancy assembled her dream team of executive talent, culminating with the hiring of Glenn Schaffer, a recently retired USAF Major General, as the president of the company.

Shortly after transitioning the presidency to Glenn, Nancy and I were having lunch. I asked her how the executive team was settling in with their new leadership. Her response surprised me.

"Running this company is great. I mean really great. I have all kinds of highly paid and highly qualified people around me. We have experts at every key position. When I chair an Executive Team meeting, I look down the conference table and see people with their own standing in the industry. They have strong reputations in their fields, and much larger companies than ours would love to have them on board. I look around, and all I can think is that if I didn't *own* the company, there is no way that these guys would choose me to be in charge!"

Reverse depression doesn't result merely from a lack of things to do. Disorientation can also come from fear and insecurity. After years of knowing what comes next, of directing all activity, the founder is uncertain of the right steps to take next. His third eye is failing.

Hiring top talent is supposed to address that insecurity, but in some ways it can magnify the sense of identity loss. As long as the owner remains the owner, however, employees will continue to look to him for leadership. Now, however, there is an added burden of knowing that a stupid decision not only risks the current level of success, but it might also reveal the emperor's missing wardrobe.

Progressives make the leap to the next level of leadership

Like others before her, Nancy made the leap from entrepreneur to CEO, but it wasn't easy. It required a new way of thinking and a new worldview. It took years, and being on unmapped ground meant she made almost as many missteps as when she was first learning to run her company. She often characterized this new journey as "learning how to hold on while letting go." Ultimately, Nancy learned how to translate her enjoyment of hands-on accomplishments into the satisfaction of leading her team as they built a much more complex organization.

Nancy's story has a very happy ending. In 2008, she sold her company for a reported $38,000,000 in cash. Some lessons are well worth learning.

Making the Leap

There is no step-by-step guide to transforming an entrepreneur into a CEO. Laying out rules and processes for chief executives would be contrary to the entire purpose of this book. You can become a CEO by doing the things you do well. You just have to learn how to function on a different level.

Each entrepreneur is different. He builds a unique company culture. If this chapter applies to you already, then you have evinced a rare blend of skills and fortitude. If it applies to you in the future, then you will have succeeded where many others failed.

If you choose to become a CEO, you will make the transition from a lifestyle to a legacy business. You need to identify new goals, both for yourself and for your organization. How you approach those objectives will be determined by your personal preferences and style, but here are a few general areas to consider:

Vision

As long as you own a company, you are responsible for its vision. As you develop into your new role, don't be surprised if your previous vision seems a bit, well, narrow in retrospect. It is hard to look down the road when your nose is to the grindstone. Now that you've developed a successful organization, what can you do with it?

Innovation

You built a machine that works, and you are the only one who can change it without getting wrapped up in the consequences. If you had never taken a risk, you would still be working for someone else. Let your managers do it by the book. Your job is to keep trying new things.

Face Time

Warren Bennis, the pioneering guru of leadership as a field of study, says that the most important role of a CEO is to be the company's liaison with other CEOs. You have the time and money to attend leadership conferences and other gatherings of successful people. Your networking should be on a completely new level.

Learning

You built a business while juggling leadership, management, technical proficiency, and accounting. Imagine what you could do given time to actually *think*. Get away for long periods regularly. Travel. Learn how things are done in other industries or other countries. You will naturally start applying what works to your own business.

Mentor

You've collected a lot of knowledge along the way. Conveying some of it to other people not only helps them, it allows you to assess it in a new light.

A last cautionary note on your transformation into a CEO. Beware of the time trap. For years, your business imposed limitations on the amount of time you could "spare." Now that you have time to "spend," there are an endless number of people who will lay claim to it. Some want you to look at their new idea, or give them advice on their bad idea. Some need your help; others know people who need your help.

It seems stingy to deny your time to those who ask. Frequently they unconsciously reveal how little they comprehend the value of your time. "I'm *only* asking for an hour."

Your time was valuable when you had so little of it to spare. Once you are a CEO, it is *more* valuable than ever before. Don't discount it, and don't let others decide how you can best use your newfound (and hard won) resource.

Chapter 17
New Hunting Grounds

EVERY BUSINESS OWNER EVENTUALLY begins to consider his or her "wealth event," the monetary realization of a lifetime of hard work. Whether you are a Creator, an Inheritor, an Acquirer, or a Technician, the biggest payoff for the risk and effort of building a business is frequently greatest when you leave.

There are only three ways to exit your business. You can sell it to an outsider, transition it to an insider, or die at your desk. That's it. The big question is whether or not you are going to act as a hunter and choose when, where, and how your business is going to pass from your control.

Outsider (third party) Sales

Most business owners have a vague anticipation of an eventual sale to a third party. When it comes time to sell, they are frequently subjected to an unpleasant wake-up call regarding the value and marketability of their businesses. There are a number of third party exit methods. Each type is limited by what you have built and how you built it.

The valuation ranges I quote below are accurate, and have remained relatively steady for years. It is common (and natural) for an owner to perceive greater value for what he built. I hear entrepreneurs attempting to justify higher appraisals based on what the company *used* to do, what it *could* do in the future, or what it *would* have done under different circumstances. None of those will add value to an objective appraisal. Acquirers look at the numbers. They pay for profit and cash flow, not what might have been. Nor will they pay extra for what they will add to the business after *you* leave.

There are legitimate ways to increase the value of your business. Remember that "The more you work in your business, the less it is worth." Your entire ownership career should be focused on making yourself obsolete. Buyers of any type will pay more for a business that has documented systems, skilled management and a history of executing according to plan without the owner's intervention. The more these features are in place, the closer to the top of each valuation range your business will be.

Here are the common valuation ranges for privately held businesses, sorted by the four types of third party buyers they attract:

Individual Operators

For small businesses, those where the owner makes a decent living by running the business on a day-to-day basis, a sale to another entrepreneur is the most common form of third party transition. "Small" is typically defined as companies with a selling price below $2,000,000, but the individual buyer market is dominated by businesses that sell for less than $1,000,000, and often for under $250,000.

To attract an individual operator, your focus should be on building the company's Seller's Discretionary Earnings (SDE). That is the broadest measure of profitability and value in a small company. You may recall from chapter 12 that SDE includes operating profit, interest on debt, non-cash flow expenses (depreciation and amortization), and any benefits the company pays for you.

The typical selling price to an individual operator is between 2.2 and 3 times the company's SDE. It is simple arithmetic. The SDE must be sufficient to provide an acceptable return on the buyer's down payment, coverage of a minimum of 1.25 times the cost of debt service, and appropriate compensation for the new owner.

More detail about preparing for the sale of a small company can be found in my book *11 Things You Absolutely Need to Know about Selling Your Business*.

Investor Buyers

If your business makes over $1,000,000 annually in earnings before interest and taxes (EBIT), it may be a candidate for purchase by investors. The most common investor buyer is a private equity group (PEG). These are professionals who assemble pools of investment money for the specific purpose of purchasing companies. There are thousands of PEGs operating in the U.S., and each has its own investment preferences.

Note that PEGs, like any buyer except an individual, will usually look at your profitability without considering extra benefits (SDE items) for the owner. They typically value using tax returns and reported profit—period.

Investor buyers expect to acquire functioning management in each deal. If you are a critical component of daily operations, this probably isn't an exit strategy for you. However, selling partial interest to a PEG can be a way to take some of your equity off the table, and strengthen the balance sheet while you prepare a successor.

Darrell Arne of Arne & Co. (Arne-co.com) tracks the prices paid by investors for small and mid-market ($2,000,000 to $50,000,000 selling price) companies, and has published **Most owners have only a vague concept of their company's value** an interesting statistic. Regardless of the economic cycle or availability of funds, PEGs pay between 4.7 and 5.2 times EBIT on average. It makes sense that their range is tight, since they are buying solely for a targeted return on investment.

Competitors

A frequent mistake made by entrepreneurs who want to sell their companies is keeping it a secret. Exiting a business is a normal part of the entrepreneurial lifecycle. Carefully managed, a competitor can be your best possible buyer.

A competitor needs little ramp-up time to learn the business, and should realize considerable economies from the combined companies. The result is often a better company with stronger management and systems. That potential increased profitability could have a major impact on your selling price.

This is where giving time to your trade or professional association can really pay off. You should know your competitors, and have a good idea of which ones run ethical, well-managed businesses. Start by identifying those with whom you see a cultural fit.

Deal with a competitor through a third party. Although I am certified as a business broker, I do not recommend hiring a broker to handle competitor approaches. Brokers are compensated by contingency fees, and may be reluctant to move as slowly as a competitor negotiation dictates. In addition, a broker's normal commission is too high a price when the owner has already identified a specific buyer. Use brokers when you need a business broadly marketed.

I recommend utilizing an attorney to make the initial approach, and to keep your identity confidential until you are sure there is a deal to be made. While a perceptive competitor can typically guess whose numbers they are looking at, they are more likely to keep the news to themselves if there is a lawyer holding them accountable for leaks.

Strategic Acquirers

Buyers who purchase a small company for strategic reasons value the business based on what they expect to do with it after the acquisition. By definition, the buyer is addressing a strategic need. Most often it is new products for their existing customers, new customers for their existing products, proprietary intellectual property (products, systems, or patents), or new geographic markets.

> Selling to a competitor is a viable exit plan

When your business is bought for strategic reasons, valuation is in the eyes of the beholder. Strategic acquisitions range from four times EBIT to ten, twelve and even fifteen time EBIT. In rare cases, profit ceases to become a measure and the price paid has little relation to normal multiples.

Many business owners hope to find a strategic buyer, just because that is the "best" buyer. They have spent their entire careers trying to outperform others around them, and expect that they will naturally do the same when it comes to finding a buyer for their company.

It rarely works out that way. Most small businesses are just not strategic. They have no chance of attracting the kind of multiples that accompany unique competitive differentiation. If you get work by being the low bidder, if you are a franchisee, if you compete on price, have a lot of small competitors, or competitors who can get into your business with little or no investment, you are probably not a strategic target.

Selling a business to a third party is not for amateurs. Just because you understand your business doesn't mean that you understand the business of selling businesses. **Selling to a third party isn't for amateurs** Approach it as you would anything else that involves high financial risk and a major change in your lifestyle. Assemble a team, including a qualified broker (if you need to find a buyer), a tax advisor, and an attorney who is experienced in transactions before you begin.

Insider Transitions

Finding outside buyers for a small business can be daunting. According to the International Business Brokers Association (IBBA), four out of every five businesses listed for sale never sell. Business brokerage is an entire industry built around a 20% success rate.

The ageing demographics of entrepreneurs in America (See my e-book, *Beating the Boomer Bust* available at TheBoomerBust. com), the disinclination of successor generations toward entrepreneurial effort (more farmers than hunters), and the increasing ability of large corporations to compete on a local level, all combine to make the sale of a small business increasingly challenging.

Unfortunately, many hunters have an exit strategy something like this: "I'll just wait until I find a young person just like me, with the same combination of skills, and a willingness to work sixty hours a week, and I'll sell him this great opportunity I built."

It's not going to happen. If your chances are four to one against a successful sale to start with, every additional qualification required of a buyer (great work ethic, understanding the industry, multiple skill sets) serves to make the odds even worse.

If you really want to control your exit schedule and price, you may want to consider selling to an insider. Family and employees offer great opportunities for an orderly exit, and often provide the best scenario for you to maintain control of the process.

Family Transitions

Selling to the next generation of family ownership is either the easiest or the most difficult way to pass along a business. It can be the easiest because you know the buyer well, and he or she knows you. Pricing is typically based on the seller's need for retirement income, balanced by the buyer's (actually the company's) ability to pay.

It can be the hardest because every financial and management decision has family repercussions. Dad and Mom have always been, and will always be, Dad and Mom. Sibling rivalry never goes away completely, and children who work outside of the business need to be considered as much as those who are involved.

If you are the founder or principal architect of the company, your tendency to be paternalistic grows exponentially when you actually *are* the father. Your hunter tendencies to make quick decisions can get you into real trouble here. With family transitions, the rule is to go slow and get plenty of buy in.

Internal sales allow you to control time and price

For entrepreneurs who have the majority of their net worth tied up in the business, the situation is even more complex. Children who aren't involved in the business deserve equal treatment when it comes to your estate, but no subsequent owner wants to split profits with shareholders who contribute nothing. I'm amazed at the number of owners who divide their company equally among children, in the incredible fantasy that filial affection will keep one sibling working for the benefit of the others over the next thirty or forty years.

In our exit planning practice, we recommend that children running the business be given ownership and control of the business. For estate purposes, they often get that ownership by "purchasing" the stock of the other children for a note. That allows their siblings to realize a fair share of the inheritance, while leaving the children who work in the business to enjoy the increases in value they create.

You should obtain a professional valuation for the business, especially if there is a question of balancing your estate among offspring. In reality, the value of the business in a family sale is based on what you need to live comfortably in retirement. Since you will be financing the purchase, (few lenders will finance family successions) you will need to balance your income needs with the ability of the business to service the debt.

Employee Sales

Every employee transfer I've worked on started the same way. I ask the owner whether he has employees who can handle running the company. He responds affirmatively. I ask why he isn't selling it to them. "Because they have no money!" is his incredulous response.

Of course they don't. Only a strategic buyer is paying real money for your company. All other buyers are simply advancing you some of the money they expect to make from the business in the future. Whether it is in the form of an earn out, a seller's note, service on a bank loan or return on investment, the purchase price of every business comes from the company's own cash flow.

Selling to an employee, or to a group of employees, is just a matter of arranging the cash flow to accomplish your objective. Done right, it can let you take the full value of your business, maintain control until you leave, and walk away with all of your proceeds on your last day of work.

Does that sound incredible? Actually, we do it every day. It takes at least three years, with five an even better time frame. It also requires some of the same cooperative thinking that a family transition takes, in order to minimize taxes and maximize your proceeds. Properly planned, a reasonably competent management team is a ready candidate for buying your business.

ESOPs

Employee Stock Ownership Plans (ESOPs) often spring to mind when entrepreneurs think about selling to employees. Most don't pursue them, because of ESOPs reputation for being difficult, complex, and expensive.

Some of that is true, but there are a number of benefits that may make it worthwhile to consider for your exit. The complexity is roughly the same as when setting up a good qualified retirement plan. ESOPs can be structured to place operating control in the hands of an individual or small group of managers. Finally, there are substantial tax advantages for the seller under the right circumstances.

A cautionary note. Poorly designed ESOPs can leave a seller liable for the company's value years after the sale. It isn't something you can do without experienced professional advisors.

The Third Alternative

Some business owners just can't live without their businesses. I once interviewed an owner in his late seventies. When I asked him about his exit plan, he responded with something that stunned me, although it was memorable.

"Son, my plan is to have the last thing I hear on this earth be the sound of my forehead hitting this desk."

Aahhh ... *okay* then! To each his own. I admire that fellow's dedication to his business, but I strongly recommend one of the other two approaches.

Chapter 18
The Next Step

LEAVING YOUR BUSINESS is not easy. Like reverse depression, it can often be confusing to determine who you are if you aren't the owner of a business. Entrepreneurs have a special brand of work/life balance. Work is their life, and their life is work.

Remember, hunters are linear. They move forward. Leaving a business can be accomplished successfully if you are excited by what comes next. If your exit planning stops at the exit, there is a higher likelihood of failure. When selling a business is the most significant financial event of an entrepreneur's career, failure isn't a very attractive option.

Phone Booth Syndrome

We all have engaged in a Superman fantasy at some time. Everyone has wished (at least secretly) for some transformational event where we suddenly become someone else, a more powerful, more personable, or wealthier version of who we are.

For some business owners, their business is their phone booth. Each day they transform into <insert hero music…ta da> *The Business Owner*, a being with powers far beyond those of mortal men or women. That persona has become an integral part of their self-perception and how they expect to be regarded by the rest of the world. After years of wearing it, they don't know how to take the Superman suit off.

Some owners don't know how to take off their Superman suit

Many entrepreneurs started out as great cold callers. They had a message, and they were evangelists in delivering it to potential customers. However, once they are comfortable in their superhero cape, they become terrible at cold calling. They are accustomed to contact with people who know who they are. Their business mixer introductions begin with "Elizabeth Martin, of Martin Enterprises." Employees, vendors, and customers are all aware that they are dealing with the decision maker, the last word on what the company will or won't do. When an owner is reduced to a common sales role, dealing with people who have no idea whom they are talking to, he finds it difficult to work without the *gravitas* of his superhero cape.

The persona of being an owner permeates everything we do, and influences all of our relationships. Your business owner aura expands to encompass your family.

A friend of mine founded an offbeat gift shop. Let's call it Square Circles for this story. He was a very clever promoter and developed a reputation for terrific marketing. At one point, the local advertising association called to tell him that his ads had been nominated for an award, and that they needed the name of his agency for the nomination. When he told them he didn't use an agency because he wrote all the ads himself, they dropped him from the nominees.

His marketing was effective, and as Square Circles became better known, he expanded to a second, third, and finally a fourth location. Unfortunately, he outgrew his cash flow and eventually the stores failed. Like many hunters, he was great at developing business, but less interested in dealing with mundane things like working capital. The failure didn't bother him much. He simply took a job while he looked for his next opportunity.

When I ran into him a little later, I asked how he was coping as a non-owner. "I'm fine," he said, "but my wife is having a difficult time of it. Everyone knew our business from its advertising. She was Mrs. Square Circles at the club. She sponsored events at our kids' schools under the Square Circles name. Although she did not work actively in the business, she carried business cards that identified her as an owner of Square Circles. Without the business, she seems unsure of who we really are."

Before you decide to begin your exit process, look carefully at who you are *outside* of your company. If you rely on your owner persona in every facet of your personal and social life, you may want to start developing a new alter ego. For both you and your family, a successful exit depends on knowing who you want to be once you surrender the phone booth effect of your business reputation.

Becoming a New Hunter

Planning for life after the business must recognize the reality of being a hunter.

I have never met a successful entrepreneur whose exit plan was based on doing nothing. Hunters do not stop being hunters just because they sell their businesses. Once, and only once, I met an owner who told me his sole objective was to make just enough money to lie on a beach and do absolutely nothing, forever. His business failed within the year.

In his book *Half-Time*, Bob Buford describes a process for a successful entrepreneur to give back to the community. I won't restate it here but one of the cardinal rules of *Half-Time* is that you need to do what you are good at. Too many former business owners are miserable because they try to start a second life as farmers.

Hunters focus on the next objective. The most important factor in a successful exit is that objective. When I interview a prospective client who wants to sell his business, "What will you do next?" is the only question whose answer can cause me to walk away.

If the answer to "What's next?" is, "I have no idea." the owner is not ready to move on. When I first started my business brokerage, I would accept an assignment to sell a business when the owner couldn't answer that question. Each time I made that mistake, we were unable to get to the finish line. The price was not quite right or the buyer wasn't quite right, or the financing wasn't quite right. In reality, the owner couldn't envision a future where he was not running the business.

The most challenging obstacle in transitioning to life after the business is personal. Self-perception as an owner becomes such an integral part of our persona that we cannot envision functioning as someone else. Our lives are so wrapped up in the business that we do not know how to fill in the gaps it leaves when we move on.

Once, our brokerage business had landed a particularly lucrative listing. A client hired us to sell a very attractive and extremely profitable business. The owner was in his sixties and already spent long periods away from the company. He knew of several large corporations that wanted to acquire his operation. Our assignment was to coordinate their offers and manage the due diligence process.

After a few weeks, we had two written offers from strategic buyers on the table, each for more than *twice* the owner's target price. It seemed that all that remained was the popping of champagne corks. Then the owner went incommunicado.

We knew he was around, but for days, he was "out of the office." He didn't answer his cell phone. Emails were unreturned.

Finally, we tracked him down by calling his mobile from a different number, so he couldn't screen us with his caller ID. He made a few excuses about being busy and then blurted out his problem.

"I wake up every morning since you presented me with the offers having the same thought. If I didn't go to my company today, what would I do? I don't have an answer. Please call the buyers and tell them my company is off the market."

That was over eight years ago. He is now well into his seventies. He still has the business. He doesn't go in every day, but he maintains an office there in case he chooses to. He does not need the income, and he has no succession plan. When he dies, his family will be well taken care of whether the business sells or not. He has made a conscious decision that the most important thing for him is wearing the cape, and being a business owner for the rest of his life.

It is a shame that so many owners sacrifice their lives, families, and even health for years in the belief that there is an event somewhere in the future that will make it all worthwhile. When that event comes, they don't know what to do with it.

Fortunately, the skills that made you successful in business are rare. There are endless opportunities to put them to good use, in your own time and on your own terms.

Hunters Hunt

Henry Ford said, "Asking why a man should be Boss is like asking why he should sing tenor in the choir."

Entrepreneurs are not smarter than other folks, although we like to think we are. We are just different. I have never met a top corporate executive who thought he made millions of dollars a year because he just *wasn't bright enough* to own a small business.

Hunters choose to do what they do because they want control. This book is about controlling your workplace, controlling your worker, controlling your work, and controlling your future. It is also about controlling yourself.

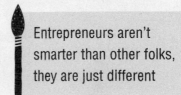

Entrepreneurs aren't smarter than other folks, they are just different

Do you remember the "Hunter's Diagnosis" from Chapter 2?

Works tirelessly in pursuit of a vision not seen by others, juggles more responsibilities than normal people can handle, able to get the big picture, sees the potential outcome of actions through multiple iterations and decision trees, carries the burden of providing not only for his own family, but for the families of those who work for him, accepts the liability of bad results as a consequence of making decisions, accomplishes massive amounts of work while understanding that he will never, ever be "caught up," functions in chaos when everyone else is panicking, has no time to waste listening to idiots, can accomplish huge projects in short time frames, able to leap mid-sized buildings with a running start.

Celebrate being a hunter. Your strengths provide the backbone of the greatest economy in history. Each point of our diagnosis is something to be proud of.

Works tirelessly in pursuit of a vision not seen by others,

Your third eye, the ability to know where you are going when others can't see the future, is the foundation for all that follows. You don't have to have hard evidence to know what is right, or what will work. Trust your hunter's instincts.

juggles more responsibilities than normal people can handle,

The farmers who work for you would be paralyzed with fear if they had to deal with the stress, the pressure and the risk of owning a business. A hunter accepts all of it as part of the challenge.

sees the potential outcome of actions through multiple iterations and decision trees,

Tenacious problem solving is your natural skill. If a plan isn't working, don't be afraid to go to plan B, or C, or X, Y and Z. You will find the solution. It is the ability that got you this far.

carries the burden of providing not only for his own family, but for the families of those who work for him,

Owning a business is hard work, but the rewards can be much more than just financial security. Take the time to look at the livelihoods you provide. You teach employees new skills, and give them the tools to improve their lives. The wages they spend help others in the community. You are the pebble in the pond of widening ripples of benefit for others.

accepts the liability of bad results as a consequence of making decisions,

Sometimes you have to bear the consequences of others' bad decisions. It is all part of the risk of being a hunter. Control that risk as much as you can, but of course you know that there is never 100% control. That's what keeps it exciting.

accomplishes massive amounts of work while understanding that he will never, ever be "caught up,"

An entrepreneur has a lousy boss. Unfortunately, he can't just say "Take this job and shove it." Don't waste a minute in self-pity for your lot in life. You *chose* it, which is a luxury that many folks can't imagine. If you were willing to let others dictate your workload, you could have been a farmer.

functions in chaos when everyone else is panicking,

Employees and family look to you for leadership. When you are unsure or afraid, remember that there is a reason why you wear the cape. Keep your management tasks simple, so that you can handle the chaos. You might be the only one who can.

has no time to waste listening to idiots,

Time is inflexible. Yours is too valuable to waste. Spend it on the things you do well, and hire other people to do the rest.

can accomplish huge projects in short time frames,

Your ADD hyperactive focus is a gift, not a liability. Use your adrenalin wisely, but put it to work on the things that bring you pleasure—creating, building, and developing new things.

able to leap mid-sized buildings with a running start.

All right, so maybe I got a bit carried away ... but you get the point.

I was lucky to be born a hunter, and consider myself incredibly fortunate to have spent half of my life working with hunters. They are heroes, and it's the most rewarding work I could imagine.

If you are a hunter, I hope this book helps you to better understand who you are; and how important your role is, even in our modern farming society. Sometimes we don't quite fit in, but we aren't misfits. We are the three percent who create two-thirds of the new jobs for all of the rest. We hunt. It is time we stopped allowing farmers to tell us that we are doing it wrong.

Good hunting.

Epilogue: The Oldest Wish in the World

The crops have failed.

First there wasn't any rain, and then there was too much. The tribe's winter food stocks lie rotting on the ground.

For many years, the harvests were plentiful. The farmers had demanded an end to the idleness of the hunters between hunts, insisting that they stop ranging for days at a time and contribute more work in the fields. Hunting became an occasional activity to put some tasty meat in the common pot.

Now the tribe's work over the summer has washed away. Facing certain starvation, they turn to Hunter. "Help us!" they beg. "Only you can secure our survival."

Hunter sharpens his blades and retips his arrows. He selects men to follow him. Some are grizzled veterans of great hunts from many years before. They will teach their skills to the younger, stronger men along the way. Some of the boys in the group look nervously at the others. They have never before been responsible for the tribe's survival. They understand that they cannot fail.

The weather has turned unseasonably cold. Days of steady rain promise difficult tracking and aching muscles. Hunter pulls his cape, the skin of a giant deer, more tightly around him. He thinks that it is a long time since he has seen a giant deer.

The tribe gathers around the hunting party. The shaman makes his pleas to forces unseen for a successful hunt, and to bring the men back uninjured. Hunter signals his men to begin the long trek to the hills, where the farmers have not yet chased away all the game.

The tribe watches as he leads his party along the trail. Hunter is almost out of sight when a single voice calls out from far behind him with the oldest wish in the world.

"Good hunting!"

Index

About the Author

John F. Dini, CBMA, CExP, CBI is a serial entrepreneur, although he prefers the term "chronically unemployable." He has signed both sides of his paycheck for over 30 years.

John has spent over 11,000 hours coaching hundreds of entrepreneurs and building one of the most successful peer advisory organizations in the United States.

Mr. Dini writes numerous articles on business topics for newspapers and magazines, in addition to his weekly online column on business ownership, Awake at 2 o'clock in the Morning? (www.awakeat2oclock.com) He speaks frequently to business groups and national associations, and is a long time member of Jim Blasingame's "Braintrust," appearing regularly on The Small Business Advocate® nationally syndicated radio program as an expert on the issues of business ownership.

John lives in San Antonio, Texas with his beautiful wife and their two sons.

You can contact him through his website at www.johnfdini.com